Oracular Marketing

How to Build an Evergreen, Predictive Online Marketing Platform for Your Business, Products and Services

By Steven Laurvick
http://www.OracularMarketing.com

AME LLC
1500 Jamielinn Lane, Las Vegas, NV 89110
steve@askame.com
1 (702) 726-7970

There is financial risk in any business venture and we ask that you consider this before investing in anything recommended within the pages of this book.

"The average outcome expected is nothing. The "average" individual will not read this book to its conclusion. The "average" individual does not take action at all, and so doesn't make a dime; thus losing money from day one, when they bought this book. Don't be "average" take action, be persistent, when one thing doesn't work do something else until you find out what does. The "average" person can achieve great success, but most will not. That is why those who take persistent action achieve success and are no longer the "average" individual."

DEDICATION

Local business owners enrich their communities in many ways. They provide much needed products and services for their patrons, jobs and stability to their employees, neighbors & neighborhoods. So this book is dedicated to the backbone of our society; the hard-working and innovative men and women who devote their lives to running the shops, factories and offices in every village, town and city!

FREE BONUSES FOR YOU

So I have a few gifts for you hard working business owners. We have a library of video tutorials we have used to teach our team to create content and build platforms online for our own and our clients businesses. We have them placed in a membership site and because you bought this book you are entitled to access to…

-Videos showing you or your staff how to quickly create videos to promote your business using Animoto, a free online tool.

-A video tutorial and pdf that gives you sample "Mandatory Pages" that should be on every website to satisfy search engine minimum expectations.

-Two videos demonstrating simple html code for creating anchor text links and making images "clickable" links to your page.

-A video step-by-step for creating a Facebook page for your business, product or service.

To unlock your membership and view or download these FREE bonuses go to:

http://www.OracularMarketing.com/Members

And enter the code "gifts"

REVIEWS:

"This man clearly knows his stuff

I have read a lot of marketing books. It's part of my job. Mr. Laurvick clearly knows what he is talking about. I found his advice regarding websites to be particularly refreshing. So many designers and marketers over-think their websites. Laurvick points out why less is often more. Thank you!"

-Everett O'Keefe

"This Book Is a Treasure Map of Marketing Systems for Success

Marketing is my business, but Systems Consultant Steve Laurvick has come from a broadcasting background and really understands the demands of today's marketing on a very deep, foundational level."

In this book, Steve explains what it takes to harness the power of Google, how to create or give instructions to create a really effective website, and how to keep it simple (this is reason to buy the book on its own), but he then explains keywords and market research, the phenomenon of localized marketing, then how to incorporate the brilliance of social marketing using Facebook, LinkedIn, and Twitter.

He doesn't stop there though, he then explains the power of using Online Directories and Online Reviews, and then explains how to automate your entire system and how to track the returns. This book is a treasure trove and treasure map all in one.

If you're serious about your business and online marketing, you'll be using this book as an instruction manual and resource guide - especially since it has a resources directory as a massive bonus!"

-Cydney O'Sullivan, Best Selling Author of Social Marketing Superstars, Quantum Leap My Life, How to Be Wealthy Now

"You need to read this book!

Steve is a super talented list building, ad promoting, SEO machine. His words and his magic super-charge your path to results! Buy this book, it will move you in ways you never thought possible."

-Niki Faldemolaei

"Fantastic book!

Here's insight into the way marketing works now. The big picture has changed people won't find me if I don't put myself on the social networks they are hanging out on and make myself visible on all the devices they might use. This is a huge help in figuring out how to spend my money on advertising." - Gary Rush

"Steve is a very talented and skilled web-based designer whose work is on the cutting edge of today's information technology. As the Grand Lodge of California's Division 9 representative for the San Diego and Imperial Counties, I recognized a need for establishing our own website to facilitate the dissemination of information on events and special programs to 27 local lodges of approximately 5,000 members. Additionally, I wanted to develop a way to network and coordinate activities with many other masonic organizations in San Diego and Imperial Counties. As a result our website SanDiegoFreemason.com is an important resource in our Division, and is gaining acceptance with an organization that prefers to do good works in the background."

James A. Kurupas, Assistant Grand Lecturer, Division IX

"After much deliberation and assessing my personal skills to re-enter the job market during the housing boom implosion in mid-2008, and while not wanting to labor at an entry level position and earning minimum wages. I decided to start the training process and became a sole proprietorship in the home inspection profession. Steve was an officer in our fraternal organization and offered his services. Before I had even received my California Real Estate Inspection Association (CREIA) Certification, the web site he built for my business and my video interviews were all over the front page of the Google search results for things like "San Diego real estate inspector" and "best home inspection company." This gave me and my business instant credibility and validation when I began offering my home inspection services to real estate professionals, investors, brokers as well as individual buyers and sellers. Steve came through and delivered for me."

John Gamache, Capstone Home Inspection Services, Escondido, CA

Steve helped me set up my Google Fan page for Shpigel Acupuncture. He quickly set up news feeds to include current articles and news in the health field so the people following me would be up to date. He was great to work with. If you have a fan page to set up, he is your guy. - Alex Shpigel, L.Ac.

"My books had been languishing with my publisher when I asked Steve Laurvick for his opinion on what could be done to market and promote them properly.

He investigated and not only provided a solution; he created a system for executing the strategy and still handles the distribution of incoming royalties from Amazon. I then asked him to publish my most recent work "In Search of Grand Master Hiram." He took my edited content and it is now available on Amazon. I'm sure that it too will soon be an Amazon best seller when Steve finishes applying his marketing magic." -John R. Heisner, Author, Coronado, California

CONTENTS

Preface

The Three Pillars of Lasting Success in Business

*Ingenuity - The head of a business must have the wisdom to recognize that the people they hire will have everything to do with the future success of any endeavor undertaken by their company. The people running the day-to-day operations of your business must be quick on their feet and able to adapt to change. They must be able to make quick judgments in a crisis, and snap decisions in an emergency had better be the right ones or it could lead to disaster. It is also true that ingenuity is needed in degrees. The bigger the problem the higher up the chain the decisions to correct the problems will be determined. Thus the higher up the ladder one goes a higher degree of wisdom and ingenuity that is required. Marketing is the cornerstone of any business, and the people in charge of marketing & advertising in your business our digital world need to be smart, flexible and able to quickly adapt the systems used to promote and sell your products and services to new or evolving technologies. You must have the wisdom to recognize the need for ingenuity as well as character and integrity in the people you hire to be on your entire team, but most especially on your marketing team.

*Character - The character of a business is a reflection of, and on the business owner. The strength or weakness of a business is determined by the character of the person who leads the team. Errors in judging the character of the people within that team will result in a weaker business, one that should perform at a higher level, or simply performs poorly and will fail unless changes are made to the membership of the team. If you have team members who lack the right characteristics to perform at a high level they must be removed from your organization. If your business is not getting the leads and sales it once did then your company is performing at a low level and the first place to start looking for a solution to your problem is in your marketing and advertising team. Your business should have systems in place that predict the problems your customers have or will have and make sure that your company is found where they look when a problem arises. If you sell red widget in Boise Idaho and you search online for "red widgets in Boise Idaho" and you aren't at the top of the page then you need a different marketing team, because whoever is in charge of marketing now doesn't have right characteristics to perform the job at a high level.

*Integrity - The ability to build a strong team with the right characteristics for future success is dependent upon the integrity of the team builder. The long term success of any endeavor begins with a desire to help people, and a continuing dedication to ethical practices. Before hiring team members it must be determined whether or not this philosophy is a part of an applicant's belief system. If your company hires an unethical team member it will make your company weaker. Eventually the unethical team member will cause damage, possibly irreparable damage to your business. The ability to consistently make more money is tied like a Gordian knot to the use of ethical business practices. If your marketing and advertising systems are using improper techniques or technology to reap short term gains, you will likely pay a high penalty that could result in the failure of your business.

So when you put together your business plan be certain to start with a foundation built on the three pillars of Ingenuity, Character, and Integrity. And then as you add members to your team be certain that they believe in and will reflect upon you and your company the positive aspects of ingenuity, character and integrity. Doing so may require more time and effort in the beginning, but will save you time, headaches, and money over the long term.

Introduction

So what in the heck is Oracular Marketing? Simply put it is an online marketing platform that:

(a) Predicts what your avatar (or ideal client) is looking for, and;

(b) Puts your business, product or service under your avatar's nose no matter where he or she is looking for what they desire or need, and;

(c) Sends them to a series of highly targeted, personalized messages that zero in on exactly how to fulfill that desire or solve that problem by taking an action that will result in an immediate purchase or lead to the purchase of whatever it is that you are selling.

It is an automated system that saves the business owner and his staff time, and delivers highly targeted prospects to his place of business, cell phone or email. The system is oracular in that it automatically will speak to exactly what the prospect is in need of and nothing more until the prospect is led to take action. It could be called the fairy dust of internet marketing as it seems to magically generate leads and sales when correctly implemented. Assuming of course it is set up for a business, product or service that people actually need.

In essence marketing in an "oracular" way is the process of predicting what problems people will have and solving them before they know that they have a problem at all. It is accomplished by implementing two key moving parts. One part delivers content to all of the channels that people search for solutions to their problems; and the other part gathers the contact information from the folks who discover themselves in need of a solution for their problem, and then automatically gives them the opportunity to resolve that problem either by being led to the purchase of a product or service, or leading them to take an action like calling a business to make an appointment.

The sales and closing strategies used in the book are evergreen. I didn't invent them I have simply been using them since the dark ages which ended in 1988 when the United States government opened up the internet to public use and CERN overlaid with the World Wide Web as public domain property. What has changed, and continues to change every day is the number of channels using the World Wide Web by which people find solutions to their problems.

Prior to laptops, smart phones, tablets, iPads and the internet which all of these devices connect to, folks had to either a. pick up a big yellow book or the classified section of a newspaper and figure out what category they might find a solution to their problem so they could squint their eyes to be able to read and write down some numbers and pick up the phone, or pick themselves up and go to a place of business and hope to shop for a product to buy that might solve their problem.

Well the Yellow Pages and classified advertising might still exist as I record this, but they are both on life-support.

An ever increasing majority of the people in this world will never use print advertising to find a solution to their problems. They will use (hold up cell phone) this or a similar device, which they will keep in their pocket or purse or somewhere within 10-feet of themselves every waking and sleeping moment of the rest of their lives, because it is the lifeline for solving their problems.

And not only has the messenger changed, the method by which the solution to any problem is arrived at has become intuitive by its nature. The method by which people search for a solution to a problem is no longer arrived at by trying to think of how a marketer classifies their problem, but rather the marketer must be predictive of a problem people will have and put their business, product or service where people will find them when a specific problem is typed into the search bar or spoken into the microphone of the device that the individual will use to ask a channel on the internet how to resolve their problem.

That is how Google, Apple, Microsoft, Amazon, eBay and

YouTube; and now Facebook, Twitter and Pinterest have changed the very nature of marketing by making the process of finding a solution painless for the end user. The middle man has been eliminated and this is very good news for both individuals and small businesses.

In "Oracular Marketing" I will outline the processes I have used and added to over the years to take advantage of the disruption caused by online search engines to the field of advertising and marketing in general. And you can become an early adapter of the same strategies and state-of-the-art technology which I have used, and now teach others to use to exponentially grow their businesses, increase their sales and do it over a shorter period time.

Now with that said I initially was skeptical of writing a book on internet marketing because of the breath-taking speed with which the online marketplace grows and changes. Initially I thought the book would be obsolete before I could even publish it.

The internet changes in a flash, books are printed and never change, right?

That was my "Eureka" moment. "Aha," said I to myself, "the very nature of publishing has already been disrupted and most people now buy e-books, books that I write and publish I have total ongoing control over. So when someone buys my e-book or paperback I can offer them an updated online edition for free, or the cost of shipping if it is a paperback version they had purchased.

I can update my e-book in on the fly and republish it with a click of my mouse. The same could be done for my paperback very quickly as well, for that matter." And more than that while the earlier printed versions will be static most of the advertising practices which I am putting into this book are tried and true "evergreen" marketing processes that will always be relevant.

In fact basic marketing principles are turbocharged by the internet as the result of the exponential increase in prospective customers it provides.

I can build trust by delivering added value.

In this book you will be shown tried and true practices that worked on flyers pulled from Ben Franklin's printing presses, to NBC's first radio broadcasts, to ABC's first television shows, to CNN's first cable broadcasts and now work on YouTube, Facebook and LinkedIn.

They are "disruption proof" techniques, and while the messenger may change the philosophy remains the same. As change occurs within the online environment we will be interactive with you our reader. You will be alerted to important elements or changes within this book by "FREE RESOURCE" boxes. These will be links to updated webpages with videos, pdfs or video tutorials where we update elements of the book related to the elements on the internet most prone to change.

Do yourself a big favor and use the "FREE RESOURCE" links. You'll be glad you did. They will save you time and build your client base. With that said understand that the difference between results that are average and results that are outstanding 99% of the time boils down to implementation. It isn't about IQ or beauty. Those who achieve outstanding results are successful because they take what they have learned and take action.

The principles and tools taught in this book work if implemented. When you read this book what you learn won't change how much you make or make your product or service more valuable. However when you take action using this information can increase your business six figures or more in a year. Money and sales are not dirty words.

If you are making more closing more sales it means that you are helping more people because you sell something that solves their problem. If you are making more money it means that your business is more stable, you can pay the employees who depend on you more money. And you can provide a better life for your family. Use what you learn here and put it to good use, and then please send me your success story so I can use it to motivate others to do the same.

Finally, a frequently asked question I get from folks is, "How in the world am I supposed to do all of this stuff?"

The answer is that savvy business owners either build their own good team or find someone who already has one. I provide a resource section to help you find competent people to assist you in implementing your online marketing platform.

Ok, let's get to it.

PS   As you work your way through this book, you will find references in some chapters to the "show number" at (619) 722-3263. As my bonus to you I offer additional resources related to the process or application being discussed. They might be video screen capture tutorials or pdf files that elaborate on what is being explained in the book. Please take advantage of these online bonus offers, they are designed to work hand-in-hand with the system and the Oracular Marketing concept being laid out for you.

You will undoubtedly want to incorporate the same sms texting model used in this book in your platform. You will be guided to the same tools used here at the end of the book.

PSS When you finish the book please call and leave a message with any suggestions or if you would like to tell me what you think of the work. Thanks for coming and buckle your seat belt. You're in for a wild ride!

1 PUTTING YOUR ONLINE PLATFORM ON SOLID GROUND: GOOGLE IS YOUR PARTNER

Hello and welcome to the Oracular Marketing community. I have put pen to paper (figuratively speaking), and this book outlines the processes I have developed and used to sell thousands of physical products, and have used to promote small businesses and their products and services.

First let me say, "Thank you" for joining the community, and let me congratulate you on taking a huge leap forward in your marketing efforts.

How so? This is so simply because most folks won't take the action required to achieve successful results. So here you are, you've made the right decision, now let me be your guide as we take the rest of this journey together. Since you are reading this you are by default someone who looks forward. You realize that Online Marketing is a game changer. It is likely that you have a successful business; you use online advertising to get the phone to ring, and you think this book will help to boost your marketing plan.

Or you might not think that the Internet can really help you much. But you are forward thinking and like to stay on top of the changes taking place in the marketing game. You know that word-of-mouth is still the best way to get business, you're in the Yellow Pages, and you're keeping the turnstiles moving.

You think to yourself: "Who searches for a local business on the Internet, anyway?"

The majority of your prospects, that's who, right now at this very second is searching for what you sell on a mobile phone, iPad or tablet, laptop or desktop computer.

The research is conclusive. Recent studies prove that fulfillment of online searches is done overwhelmingly by people looking for a local product or service.

A 2010 study by BIA/Kelsey and research firm ComStat found that a staggering 97% of consumers research their purchases and local services online before they fulfill them at a local business. Add that to their mid 2012 report predicting that, "By 2016, the firm expects mobile local search to exceed desktop local search by more than 27 billion annual queries," and you can see the future of your business is in the pocket book, pants or shirt pocket holding the cell phone or tablet.

This isn't so only for local search either. Disruption of the marketplace is happening to the big boys too. Fortune 500 companies like Radio Shack, JC Penny, Barnes & Noble, to name just a few are now former Fortune 500 companies fighting to stay out of bankruptcy. And yet e-retailers are often beaten out by customers who research products online but elect to make the purchase at a shop where they live. Clearly a large percentage of shoppers like to be engaged personally, they get value out of the "human touch;" they determine what they want online, but in the end they want to hold the item in their hand and be taken by the hand by a sales person before they will buy.

Clearly what that means is that a business without (or with an insufficient) online platform is simply not going to be found at all. Consumers prefer to fulfill their internet searches locally, so if your business, product or service doesn't show up while a prospect is searching online for what you sell, for all intents and purposes you don't exist; that prospect is going to walk into the door or call the business who has that Online Platform in place.

This is disastrous for the local business owner who has shunned the Internet (or that has an ineffective online marketing strategy).

This isn't being alarmist, it's a fact: most of your potential clients are looking for whatever it is that you sell online, in fact they prefer online search to traditional media like the Yellow

Pages because it is easier and faster. In fact, a recent 2009 study by ComScore and TMP Directional Marketing showed that, for the first time, the number of clients searching for local businesses on the Internet exceeded that of the Yellow Pages. In a 2013 BIA/Kelsey report they predict that, "the U.S. Yellow Pages industry will cross over into majority digital status in 2016, with $2.7 billion of $5.3 billion total revenue coming from non-print sources." By 2017, BIA/Kelsey, "expects the projected $5.1 billion U.S. Yellow Pages industry to be 56 percent digital." Simply put, people don't use the Yellow Pages anymore, because online search is intuitive and a more convenient way to get what they want or need.

For those of us who grew up with three television stations and no internet this can be difficult to believe, but consider your own changing habits and you will recognize the truth of it: When was the last time you looked for something in the Yellow Pages? Did you go find the book and let your fingers do the walking? Or did you go to your computer and look for whatever it was that you wanted or needed? Even if you so still prefer the Yellow Pages watch your kids, friends, and family. How many of them use the Yellow Pages or want ads in the local paper? Serious study will make it clear that people do not look for what you are selling in the same way they used to.

Surprisingly many businesses still have huge portions of their budget devoted to the Yellow Pages and print advertising. Many local business owners allocate $30,000 or more to their Yellow Page advertising budget alone, something that in our time is simply throwing money out of the window; Traditional print media delivers diminishing returns to their clients.

Advertising dollars will reap exponentially greater returns if properly used to build an Online Platform. Those businesses that track return on investment (ROI) from print advertising campaigns, and I mean every one of them, see sales results turning down sharply.

Savvy business owners are fleeing traditional advertising venues and switching into internet marketing campaigns. The internet has supplanted traditional print media advertising, and the internet is not only here to stay, it is going to be in everyone's pocket very soon! An effective Online Platform isn't a fly-by-night strategy, it is the future and the future is now. If you are not implementing an Online Platform then I'm sorry but as Hemingway said, "Perchance he for whom this bell tolls may be so ill as that he knows not it tolls for him." But fear not! It is not too late.

The good news is that if you are reading this you already have or soon will be implementing a powerful online presence that will put you on top of your local search engine results.

CAUSE FOR PAUSE: How does this affect you?

Just exactly how do you get your business, product or service into this search results minefield? I mean seriously, aren't major corporations throwing millions of dollars at the internet to gobble up all the top spots for search terms? How can local businesses hope to compete in this complicated and confusing online marketplace?

Guess what, you can. Google is on the side of the local business owner because their job is to give people what they are looking for when they search for something they want or need. To that end Google has made major changes to their search algorithm to provide just that; they have moved search results for brick and mortar stores to the front page of search results using "Local Search Return" and an application called "Google Places / Google + Local," this was previously only found on Google Maps and now it has been merged with overall web search when people type in a request to find a product or service.

What exactly is local search return? Local search return is very good news for local businesses who find and use it. Previously, when someone went to Google Maps to find something, local businesses would populate a map in the city the where that person was searching for it. If that person searched "NY, NY", for example, an interactive map would appear with markers pointing to businesses that fit the search description on the map, they show local places of businesses that were nearby.

The hospitality industry (restaurants, hotels, bars) were quick to take advantage of this application and have and continue to make gobs of money with it, and those who haven't have been experiencing dramatic losses of business; travelers have to find places to eat and sleep, so the Google Maps local search return feature is highly effective for both businesses and their customers because it shows users instantly where to find 5-10 local businesses where they are going, and the business phone number so they can choose and book the room or reserve a table thus facilitating an offline sale.

The results of this quickly made it clear that other local businesses would benefit in exactly the same way that restaurants and hotels have, and began listing themselves on the local search return maps as well.

The folks at Google realized that since people were using their Maps Search Application to find what they required, then certainly users are also searching on "regular" or Web Search too, but not understanding that at that time the user had to go to the Maps Search section to obtain local business search results.

So at that point in time, Google's Web Search page would return a list of keyword relevant web pages as search results; the search page didn't show or offer the map-based local businesses and so users were not getting what they were looking for, and so Google set up the Local Search returns to effectively merge Map Search with Web Search, the regular search page, when someone is looking for a local business or service.

When you want to find a product or service on Google now, it returns the regular search page AND a map with up to seven marked businesses on it which are all local businesses.

This is a gold mine for business owners who take advantage of it, since now they have not only a real chance to compete by getting onto the front page of the search engine results, but they can also be at the top of the first page of the search results in the Local Business Search area. Until very recently it was almost impossible for local businesses to compete on a national

level with 800-lb gorillas like Amazon or Walmart. Now you can

compete and you can win.

 You can put your business on Google Places and you can take

the steps to get your business to show up in the top three

results on a Local Search page search result, something that will

without question increase your business, and it's something

that didn't exist until a couple of years ago.

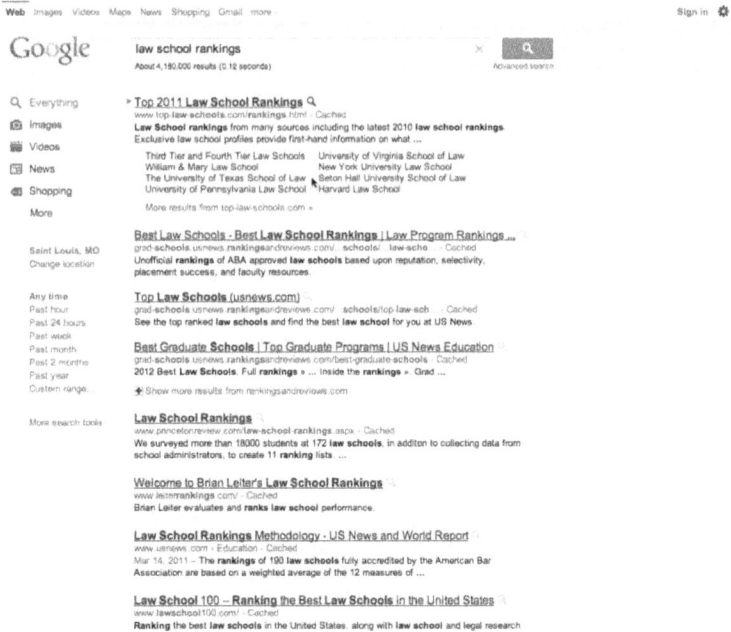

This image is a dramatic illustration of the powerful results that Local Search returns. Previously, you had little chance of competing by getting onto and remaining on the first page of Googles search results for anything; now, local business owners have the ability to put their business, product or service on top of the local search results in their area.

Granted, it's not a one step process to get to the top of the results; in most cases there are many other businesses vying for these same spots, to just have a website up with some competitive keyword phrases will not be enough (FYI, a bad website will ensure that your site will never be seen by anyone searching Google for what you sell). There is a systematic process, a blueprint so to speak, and if you follow it diligently, do the work carefully, and implement all of the instructions here in this book you will have an Online Platform that gives you the ability to hit one or all of the A, B, or C spots on your local search return!

BEWARE

Earlier you were informed that Google had changed its search algorithm. Part of that change was to deal with duplicate content (copying and pasting the same content into multiple web pages); this practice will have serious negative results to the ranking of your website if used! Google repeatedly has made it known, both by executives and company spokespersons verbally, and in print, that the goal of Google is to reward real honest-to-goodness local businesses that give quality and provide a substantial product or service to offer to the community they live in. To that end they are taking extreme measures when dealing websites that appear to be trying to "cheat" or "game" the system. They perceive as shady automation tools that spin the same content into multiple articles to post on as many websites as possible or those who create fake listings. Google will "sandbox" or delisted sites they believe are using those practices from Google's search index, and possibly forever. At first this might seem harsh or unreasonable, but you need to remember that you use Google's product and are a part of its ecosystem for free. You are able to take advantage of their tools because they allow you to. They make money by providing people with exactly what they want on whatever device people are using so that advertisers will pay to be in those same results. Their job is to make the user experience better and this benefits you both as a user and as a business; it is in your interest to have them weed out the scammers and spammers in order that you, a real business owner, can offer value and quality to consumers, and make room for your business to rise to the top when people search for your products and services.

You must also be skeptical of marketing salespersons who tell you this is a simple process! It is not and never will be easy. You will be told that it's just a matter of keyword phrases, and they will sell you content and ask you to pay them to put it on your own and many other websites. This is now a recipe for disaster. The final product is almost always reworded, reorganized or just plain copied material that will not only be worthless, but might get remove any chance your site will be on the first page of Google's search results when they figure out what you or your marketing people are doing. Don't fall for the pitch because while they may get you short term results they can show you, shortly thereafter you will fall not only off of the first page, but possibly off of the search results altogether, and you'll be lose ground to your competition by trying to take the easy way out.

Creating quality material has been and will always be the starting point for building an Online Platform and ultimately achieving success when using the internet to promote your business. Generating top-notch content isn't necessarily difficult, however it will take time, patience, and discipline. There is a blueprint here that you can use to be certain that you are generating quality content of the right kind. Content that will get you top rankings on Google!

Spammers and scammers have been gaming the system with duplicate content and link farms pretty much since the inception of the internet, but Google is the juggernaut that it is because they realized that to give people what they were looking for on a search required them to identify and eliminate those pages from their search results. Obviously they were right, and the slick tricksters are rapidly disappearing from the search engine landscape. Don't let yourself be scammed by any of these types of offers – as the old adage goes if it seems too good (or easy or cheap) to be true, most likely it is! Ask for samples of their work and read it, ask them to show you actual first page results and check out the results, if it is duplicated, rewritten, or appears anywhere else; if the salesperson won't give it to you without hesitation show them the door!

But you either haven't bitten on that pitch or have already been burned by one of those other companies; because you bought this book. Within it you are about to discover the systems and processes you need that with some time, effort, patience, and planning, will get put your business, products and services at the top of the search engine results for your area!

THE PLAIN TRUTH IS:

* Online marketing is no longer optional. Smart phones, tablets & desktop computers are where people find businesses, services and products they need: You MUST leverage the internet!

* Search is the 800 pound gorilla right now in Internet marketing. You MUST make sure your business shows up high on the list of results when users search for what you sell!

* Be cautious about how you insert your business into the

search engine marketplace! A poor presence online is worse than no presence at all

* When you need help, be wary when selecting marketing services! Old school marketers use methods that are now considered "black hat" by Google and other search engines. They may also use devious tricks to temporarily give you a boost in the search rankings but such methods will inevitably bring down severe penalties from the search engines for breaking their rules!

CHAPTER ONE BONUS: Your business isn't listed on Google Places? Text **#GOOGLEPLACES** to our book number (619) 722-3263 for short video tutorial on getting your company into Googles Local Business Search Engine.

2 DON'T LET A DESIGNER OVERBUILD YOUR WEBSITE: JUST REMEMBER "KISS"

Now we understand the enormous value Google provides to us; we have given an overview of the changes that help local businesses compete in search returns, and Google ranking in general, game changers to your marketing efforts. We understand that traditional print advertising model has been disrupted forever, and that if you expect your business, product or service to be found you are going to have to start using search in your business starting now!

But hold on. Implementers will be thinking that they need to jump away and get a website (if they don't have one) or to jump away and find someone to get it ranked. Stop! The website for your business is as an integral part of this process, and to get sales conversions from your online search marketing efforts you need a solid site that satisfies the needs of your business as well as the needs or desires of your customers.

This first step is more often than not the downfall of most small business owner's online marketing efforts. Website creation is a counter-intuitive process, less-is-more far more often than not. Web designers are more like artists than marketers. They want to sell you the latest whiz-bang, flash-pop-up playing newest gizmo available so they can play with it and show how state-of-the-art of a website they can build and show off to their next victim, err business owner.

 So now everyone tells you your site must have interactive menus, drop-down interfaces, and other assorted knick-knacks, tic-tacs and bric-a-brac. I'm telling you these gadgets turn your website into a white elephant. Web developers will try to push Flash this or Web 2.0 that on you, telling you how important these applications are and how much more professional your site will look. You will be tempted, but you must not believe them.

Take this to the bank; the truth about websites is this: for the typical small business and ultimately the ROI from resultant conversion rates, all of that flashy stuff does not matter. In fact it can hurt. Putting flash video pop-ups on a website means your prospect must be on a device capable of opening and playing the pop-up video.

If your site doesn't load fast enough because you have all this garbage loaded onto it, or the site isn't compatible with mobile devices, your prospect will never see your page because it won't open and he's already moved on to the next search result (who most likely is your competition). KISS or "Keep It Simple Stupid" really does apply to your website.

Clean and simple sites that are easy on the eyes and put only the information your client is interested in finding out (like your company name, phone number, address and what you sell) will work far better at boosting your conversion rates and helping your customers communicate with you. As I said it is counter-intuitive our "style over substance" culture, but it's a proven fact: simple websites have, been A/B tested with the busier, flashier sites most web designers want to sell you and the results are conclusive. You will have far better results if you use a simple, easy to read website page with the right elements and call to action.

The customers will be calling you as long as you give them what they are looking for AND your website opens on whatever device they are using, quickly.

So this may seem kind of overwhelming. Considering how much I've been going on about the necessity of getting listed properly. And that is a fact: getting ranked high on Google Search is the Holy Grail; the single most important element in online marketing.

In fact, most of the chapters in this book are devoted to achieving that result for your business. Your website, however, is an important link in the chain. However by no means is a website the most important link, not even by a long shot; the site needs to be put together correctly and look good, if not it has the potential to derail any effort to get it to the top of the search results. All that should matter to you is this: if a prospective client doesn't ring up your phone number or send you an email, all of the other work done to send traffic to your site will have been wasted.

So forget gizmos and gadgets, new, latest and greatest, flashy & fancy apps to add to your site. How up-to-date your website is makes no difference at all if it doesn't bring in business, just remember KISS!

CAUSE FOR PAUSE: What is A Good Website & How Does it Look?

The logical next question: so the artsy, highly stylized websites aren't the way to go, what is? Is there a secret to getting visitors to pick up the phone and call when they see my website?

OK here are a few elements to use. Let's go over them so you can discover how to keep it simple AND build your site so that it will get the most visitors to pick up that phone and call your office, or opt into your list, or send you an email asking for your help!

Structural Elements of Your Website: Building an Evergreen Site that Converts Leads and Sales

Believe it or not, but believe me when I tell you that in general, there is a rule which should always be used to maximize conversions from websites that are found in the search engines: The less artsy and complicated the website is, the more conversions you'll get from it.

That's right; KISS is the rule, "keep it simple stupid!" Simple, well organized websites that open on any platform or device quickly will be far more effective for your business.
Understanding that less-is-more let me make it easy for you

with this generalization of what your website layout could end

up looking like:

- Home page

- Blog

- About

- Contact

- Website Terms of Use

- Privacy Policy

And there you have it.

Nonplussed aren't you, seems kind of skimpy doesn't it? WAY

smaller than the majority of the websites you've been on, and

that's for sure; but those websites belong to someone else. You

have a lean, evergreen conversions machine of a website. Your

site was built for the sole purpose of getting prospective clients

who see it to take an action; be that to buy something, or to call

your business to buy something, or to accept an offer to join

your list so you can sell them something they need later on

down the road. More than that is a waste of time and money or worse, more flash might mean they never see your message at all; and while it might be nice that people ooh and awe over how nice you site looks if they don't buy anything or you didn't get a phone call or you didn't get them take your offer to get them on your list what difference does it make.

To you it doesn't matter if they visited or not unless they took an action when they came, an action that leads to you providing a product or service that they need. If they come to your fancy site and it doesn't open fast enough or they can't find your phone number it's a lose-lose situation, period.

Rule No. 2: Every landing page must include a call to action. A call to action is something to get visitors to call, text or email you right away. We will thoroughly discuss this critical element "call to action" below in a separate section, but be aware that for local business websites we recommend, at a minimum, the banner or header on each page has your phone number in the top-right or middle-right hand side.

A/B test studies prove, and my experience confirms, that the eye gravitates toward the right side of a page. Don't believe me? Look where Google puts ads in their own search results. A best practice is to insert a form beneath the top phone number to sign up for your newsletter, coupons, or podcast to provide an incentive for people to opt into your list by giving you their phone number and email address.

This is only an example; certainly you will likely have additional pages to add depending on your business, you may want to add a page about upcoming events you are hosting, or recent news and press about your business. Know, however, that this basic layout works extremely well, and is evergreen (meaning it always, always will work) remember, KISS: the less fancy the page, the better the results!

BEWARE:

Do not confuse less flashy with poor design. Your business and website must maintain a solid, professional look and I am advocating that you use a clean simple design.

In fact we strongly feel that having less 'flashiness' to a website often leads to better visual design as there is less clutter, and better visual design also helps with conversions. Your business may already have invested in working with a branding agency to help create a logo and a set of colors that represent your "brand", carry those into your website.

FREE RESOURCES:

Color Combos - http://www.colorcombos.com

Colour Lovers - http://www.colourlovers.com

These sites provide color palette tools. Enter the core colors you use for your business logo or ad copy and the software will suggest complementary colors for you to use on your site.

Time is money and very likely your time is better spent doing your job then building a website, you are a professional in your community and what you provide is valuable – don't make your website give potential clients the wrong impression.

So while you will likely hire someone to do the job all you have to do is follow the advice here and spell out just exactly it is that you want. Have the content ready for the web designer (images of you, your business, logos, mission statement, contact information, boilerplate for the Privacy and Terms of use pages NOTE I will give you those boilerplates at the end of this chapter.)

BEWARE: Do Not become hostage to your web designer!

I highly recommend that your company purchase the web address from Godaddy.com or similar company. In effect when you select and click the buy button you rent rather than own that URL, but you need to keep control over it. You will then need to choose a host (I do not recommend hosting with Godaddy, but you can). Hosting services should not be expensive and it is a simple matter to forward your domain name server (DNS) information from Godaddy to any Hosting Company.

www.just5buckshosting.com (up to three URLs, unlimited subdomains for all three $60 a year) Hostgator.com (excellent customer service), BlueHost.com (popular for price and service), and many more. The hosting business is fluid and cloud based systems are changing the game, but the three above and Godaddy have been around a long time and will likely be around for a long time as well.

Secondly make sure your web designer puts your website on a cloud-based platform. In plain English that means you want to have control over your website once it is built and not have to rely on whoever you hire to maintain or change it. What if your web design company goes out of business? What if your guy does shoddy work and you have to fire him. Keep control of your project by having it set up on a Wordpress.Org or similar platform. The key is that it be a cloud based system that allows for fast and easy access to the working side of the website to add new content and make changes on the fly.

With free systems like wordpress.org there are hundreds of templates and plugins (both free and paid) that make it flexible and easy to set up and use, but most importantly, once your site is set up you or whoever you hire to manage your site will always have the ability to make changes or take back control from a disgruntled employee or fired web designer.

Now, let's break down each of these pages more in-depth!

Home Page

While the "About" page will have your company story and mission statement you can use this page to hit the highlights of what services or products you provide. Bullet points are visually compelling and can give a quick overview to tell your visitors whether or not they have come to the right place, but the primary function of the "Home" page is to connect your reader with the rest of the site. It should be easy to read (no dark colors with dark lettering and use font sizes large enough to read, I also recommend using fonts like Times New Roman or Georgia that people are used to reading), has a blurb about you, and invites the reader to explore more of the site. Above all, however, make absolutely sure that the home page features your blog prominently!

The blog will be used to automatically post company news, coupons, specials, newsletters, videos, press releases and more to your Facebook Page, take blurbs to your Twitter Feed and do much, much more as time goes by. The blog serves as the auto feeder to your social network (which we will go into much more detail on later in the book).

There are different ways to promote the blog on the Home Page, if you built the site on a Wordpress.org platform your site already is a blog. And a blog is just a website that lets you do more things than a static website. It will also make it easy to make sure your website will be seen and look good on any device by simply installing the right plugins when it is set up

(I will give you a list of the best plugins to install on setup and video demos of the process of creating and setting up a WordPress site). If you choose another route think very, very carefully about how to prominently integrate your blog with the home page.

Video should also be on the homepage. A/B Test Studies have shown increases of 30% in conversions when a prospect watches a video of someone from the business on the homepage. Yes, that is 30%. Incorporate a small, short (90 seconds – 2 minutes) video somewhere on your home page. Naturally the message given in the video will affect the results you achieve, but a simple, "thanks for coming" and "here's what we are about" story works very well, it doesn't have to be a slick production video, but what you say in the video will be all important. Solve the visitor's problem, he or she found you because he or she was looking for what you are selling.

Using copy on your home must be kept to a minimum. It should address no more than 3 things:

1. Explain to them what benefit they will get by using you or your company, product or service. Don't tell them what you do, tell them what problem you solve for them.

2. Invite them to join and interact in your community by explaining what benefits they get by subscribing to your blog/social media/podcast/subscriber list and give them links to go join or visit and engage.

3. Call to action – in effect this is a bribe to get them to give up their email or phone number. You offer them something of value and they get it by opting in one way or the other. (Special offers, special reports, video tutorials, checklists, etc.)

These three elements are vital to the success of a website and the campaign behind it. So critical that we actually write the copy for these sections for our clients and place them word-for-word.

Blogs & Blogging

Blogs and "blogging" is generalized and misunderstood by most business owners. A blog is an interactive website that communicates with your client by interacting automatically with the place your client spends time. That place might be Facebook, Twitter, or LinkedIn; or it might be YouTube or Google Hangouts, or Yahoo or DailyMotion or Reddit or myriad other places that will be invented and important this year and forever into the future. The key element that makes a blog special is that it has an army of developers creating applications to communicate with existing and new social networking, video and directory websites. They are working for you and your business day and night in every corner of the globe!

The blog, in particular the Wordpress.org blog is here to stay and it is a lynchpin of any solidly built online marketing system. It is one of the tools that enables you and your business seem to be oracular or seemingly always wherever your client or prospect is looking for you anywhere they look for a solution to their problem, and it is seemingly alchemical to you in that it automatically takes your submissions and sends it to all of the other places your clients spend their time. You, or your employee, need one click of the mouse instead of 100 or 400 or 1000 copy and paste and send actions every time send a post. It is vital and it is evergreen as long as you don't abuse it.

It provides two things that are requisite to marketing success on the internet.

1. Your blog is the home to new and relevant content to your prospects and clients. You or your outsource team will discuss many things that will talk to the problem or problems your prospects and clients need solved. Entries to the blog will mostly be entered post production using automation tools, and should always include a way for the visitor to have his problem solved by taking an action with your company or on the blog post page. But you should be monitoring your posts for questions and answer them. Some of these comments

will turn into sales, a high percentage if you've built things correctly, but only if you follow up quickly.

2. A finely tuned blog will also provide new and relevant content for Google, Bing and other search engines. They are ravenous beasts these search engines and as long as your website was correctly set up with a sitemap and a logical link structure the search bots will come every time you post an item. They feed on unique, relevant content and if you build it right and feed your blog they will come, and most importantly they will rank content about you and your business if the post has value to prospective eyeballs they send to your site.

    The goal is to get your company to the top of the search engine rankings in your community, region, or state. By talking about your business, service or product and including the specific locations your clients are looking for you is a natural selection of keywords that the search engines will pick up as relevant to what your client is searching for if he or she is in your area. In other words Google knows and Siri already know where the client is, they don't have to bother typing in the city they want something on their Android or iPhone; but you do.

Your job is including your location in each post so Apple and Google and Bing know not only what you sell but where you sell it. It's worth hiring an intern to post about things going on in your local community. This will make it clear to the search engines which community, town, or city your business does business in.

This is the secret sauce you might say and it is simple to implement; often marketing agencies make this part more complicated than it really is. Marketing gurus go on and on about keyword density, latent search algorithms, and split testing.

This is another example of KISS, just pay a work at home mom, or intern or set up an outsource worker program and have them religiously post news items and calendar events on your blog about your local community! Make sure they plug your business and add assorted blurbs about what you do or sell along with a phone number and website address.

Write about what you know about, write about things that provide value to your readers: the two most obvious are your area and events going on in your community and nearby communities. If you hear someone talk about keyword density, just run away: it's likely that they're just trying to make it sound complicated to pick your pocket.

Over the years, I have discovered many things that just don't change when it comes to online marketing and human behavior. Even though I know that consistent blogging is important, getting my clients to spend their time writing twice a week is simply not a valuable use of their time.

The good news is you really don't need to.

Content creation can be done in advance and submitted automatically over time on a daily basis for you. Then the addition of an intern or outsource worker to submit generic material with your community info, and to go find content or groups on Facebook and Twitter and LinkedIn and Pinterest to spread goodwill and links to your blog and social media pages is all you need.

The "About Us" Page

Fortunately for you the "About Us" page is rarely done well by

businesses.

The reason for this is simple, they didn't give the web designer the right material to set it up right, because they don't realize how important this page is. The typical About Us page has a short blurb about the business, or about the products or about the owner, it may or may not have a map pasted on the page. This is laughable.

Why in the world are you spending your time and money on a website if you don't address the pressing needs of your client. The internet is where people find what they need and they expect their search to send them to someone who can fix that problem NOW. I don't mean tomorrow!

And if you don't tell them loud and clear that they came to the right place when they come, they are gone. If they have an overflowing toilet at 2AM they want a plumber who will come now. If your page says hi I'm Bud the plumber and I've been working North Fork my whole life and I have 6 kids and 12 grandkids... that simply doesn't cut it for Mr. & Mrs. South who have a flooded bathroom at 2 in the morning. Your About page needs to address the need, and preferably the most expensive need of your prospect. You are, "Bud's 24-Hour Emergency Plumbing Service. If you have an emergency call now 1-555-867-5309 and we will roll!"

You spent time and money to drive your business to the top of the search results and that is the first element of the magic of the internet and search. When someone has a problem all they have to do is type or now just say what the problem is, Google or Siri will listen and send them to up to seven local businesses that theoretically can solve that specific problem NOW. If they go to the first result and they don't seem to have EXACTLY what they need, they hit the back button and go to the next one.

By setting your page up to address the problem you know the searcher is going to have you are "Oracular" you knew what they were going to need before they had the problem, your webpage said you can fix that exact problem right now, and they are going to use your service or product right now.

Even better when the Search Engine records this action they know you solved the searchers problem because of the time spent and action they took while on or clicking on a link on your page, and they will reward you by moving your page or listing up in the search results. This is not rocket science, it is engineering.

You have to examine your marketplace, predict what people will need and what words they will use to solve that problem, and then send them to a page that solves that particular problem right then. There is more. You can take this to the next level by taking more general problems or broader regions and narrow them down using tools that I will discuss later in the book. But that is the magic of the internet and why online search has decimated the Recording Industry, Publishing Industry and Traditional Print Advertising like the Yellow Pages and Classified Newspaper advertising.

People use their smart phone to search for a problem because it is always within 3 feet of wherever they are. It is a security blanket and when they have a problem they go to it straight away to find a solution. When they pull up a search result and find your page they do not give a whit about your years of experience as a plumber or landscaper or water removal service when their house or yard is being flooded, they want to know if you can fix the problem by coming to fix it immediately.

This brings us to the concept of the *unique selling position-* why do clients call you instead of your competition and when you have done your job why will they want to work with you?

The "About Us" page should also include stories and testimonials about you, your business, why you're better. Pictures of you and your kids or employees and so on doesn't cut it—you have to show them why you're a step above your competition, and why they would want to work with you and not the other guy.

Your business will be picked only if you tell her or him how you will fix a particular problem, not if you tell him about your degrees, titles, or positions.

What your prospect wants to know is if you can solve his or her problem, and solve it fast and professionally. THAT is what needs to be on the "About Us" page of your website.

Just remember, KISS, instead of bragging about you, use the words on your page to explain to them how they will benefit when they choose you to solve their problem.

Take this advice to the bank, by taking this advice you will set your website above (literally above) most of the local businesses who get themselves ranked on the search engines: Either they don't tell the visitor that they do what the visitor needs or they don't set their business, product or service apart from the competition.

By default all you have to do is put the right words on the page, predict and project a quick resolution to their problem and instantly move up on the competition on the search results as well as improve your conversion rate.

The "Contact Us"

The Contact Us page should be just that and nothing more. Include your company email, phone number, and a map to guide them to your business. That's all it should be, that's all they want to know.

 You reword your call to action on this page, but this page should be clean, simple, and not distract the reader from taking action by picking up the phone or putting in their email. A contact form on this page is acceptable, but the most important thing is to provide a clear phone number and/or email address that is directed and answered by an actual human.

TIP: Go to Google Maps and put your business address in. Copy the link to the map and post it on the page. Apply the link over the words, CLICK HERE FOR GOOGLE MAP.   Make it in a LARGE font.

The Privacy Policy & Website Terms of Use Pages

These are necessary legal pages that should be included on every website.

They DO NOT need to be made highly visible, and they can be made as sub-pages and not shown on tabs or sidebars on the website.

I am not a lawyer and I do not give legal advice. You should talk to your lawyer about privacy policy and website terms of use related to your website and business before using any templates or advice given to you in this book.

That said I have made boilerplate Privacy Policy & Website Terms of Use page copy available for you to download, amend and use in your site; as well as the video tutorial created and used by my outsource work team for creating and putting them into our sites.

Use the Oracular Marketing campaign phone number (619) 722-3263 and text **#MANDATORYPAGES** to receive the copy and tutorial video.

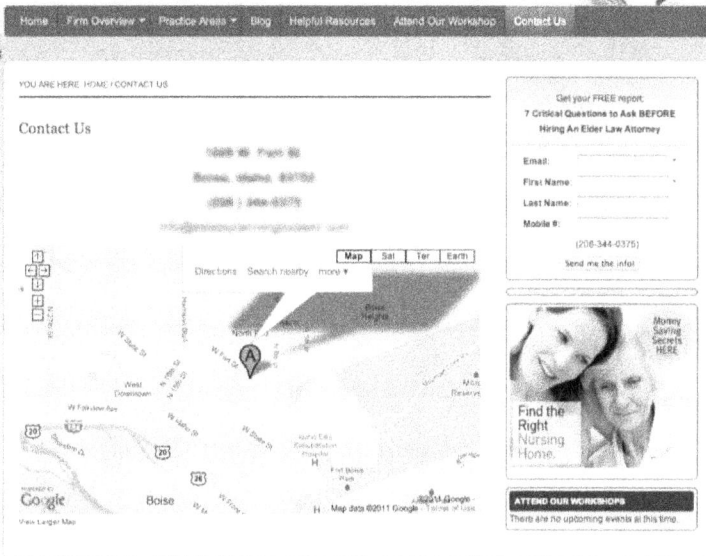

CAUSE FOR PAUSE: Understanding the "Call To Action"

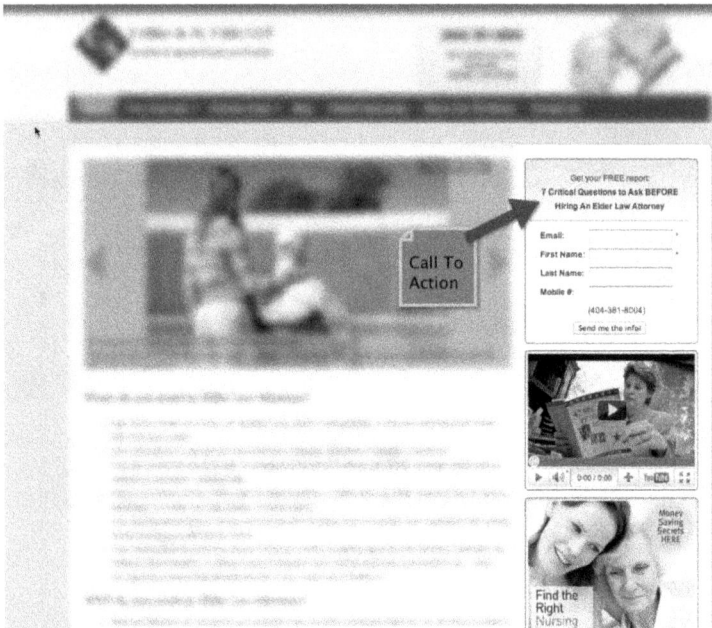

Alright the nuts and bolts of the site are now understood. You need a "URL", a host, and then you need to make a handful of pages with the right stuff on them. Let's examine the most important element of the right stuff on any webpage that is built for the purpose of connecting a buyer with a seller; specifically a call to take an action by every viewer of your webpage.

This "call to action" is simply a directive. Don't be timid, visitors want to be told what to do to resolve the issue they came to your website to fix. A call to action is simply words on a page telling the viewer to do something. Those words might be written or in an audio or video on the page.

If she has come to the page it is because she has a problem. Your business has a webpage that is designed to help the visitor solve that problem and the sooner the better as far as the visitor is concerned.

If you don't set your site up to solve that problem you haven't done your job, you've helped no one and in fact thrown your time, effort and money away; not to mention wasted your visitor's time! (The visitor's time, by the way, is actually more important to know than anything else if you want to understand how Google decides which pages move up, and which pages move down in their search results.)

An effective call to action will get a prospect to pick up the phone and call straight away.

An effective call to action might also get a prospect to text their email to get something, or enter their email address to join your community, or get your prospect to like your post on your business fan page.

It's crucial that your call to action is specific and gives them something of value in return. Again they came to your page because you were predictive in setting up your page for them to find.

The prospect is on your page because they were looking for what you sell. The next step is to understand that asking for information is a sensitive subject, and most people won't do it unless they trust you or you give them something.

Folks are savvy about spam, they know about scammers, and they're not going to give out their cell phone number or email address to typical sites they find on the Internet. You will overcome that objection and get them to give you their information.

The easiest way is to offer something special for providing information or calling now – like a big discount on a service. However, we've found that the way that works BEST is to provide a special report about something that will be very helpful to the consumer who found you by searching for the business, product, or service you provide in your area.

Examples: "Special Report: 5 dangerous things you need to know before ever hiring or calling a termite extermination company," or "4 tips for choosing a contractor for your kitchen remodeling project." or "3 outrageous myths you shouldn't believe about lumbar pain treatments provided by Chiropractors."

It is important that these examples be specific to your product or service; imagine a bulls-eye on your office door; be concise and to the point, "I have this solution to your problem and if you call this number we will make an appointment and fix your problem right away."

You should also make it clear to search engines where your business is, for example "4 things you need to know before hiring a Cowboy in Butte, Montana".

These examples will likely be strong enough to get someone to put in their email; they might say, "Hey, wow, what are those three things? I was ready to get moving and hire a cowboy tomorrow, but I better know this before I do anything" and then pop in their email and now you can quickly follow up with them (and then segment the replies and automate the follow-up responses to Cowboys who herd Steers vs Cowboys who herd Buffalo).

While I make light of it be assured that this content is vitally important, so much so that for our clients, we write this report for them and insert it into their webpage. This is simply an offer, and well written copy will convert if you have qualified prospects looking at it. It is a must that you now not just ask for a prospect's email, but for their cell phone number as well.

The world has gone mobile in short order and smart phones make the internet your oyster. Get the mobile number. AT&T was broken up years ago and they are now a what? They are a cell phone service provider.

Folks use their cell phone as their primary or even only phone number now, and so they willingly give it out to people who ask if they have are asked.

By taking all of these steps, those visitors who submit an email address or cell phone number will be a "warm" lead.

A "warm" lead is someone that needs what you are selling and a "warm" lead is going to be easier to convert into a client, ALL leads like this will be "warm" leads because you didn't solicit them, they found you!

You made sure Mr. or Ms. Searcher would find you when they had the problem you solve, they looked for a solution to their problem, Google or Bing or YouTube or Facebook or Amazon or Apple or eBay recognized you as the solution to Mr. or Ms.

Searcher's problem and those channels were nice enough to show YOUR page to Mr. or Ms. Searcher — that's the magic of online search, you have a qualified lead and all you have to do is close Mr. or Ms. Searcher and make the sale. However if you don't act quickly it'll be that much harder to close the deal. And that my friend brings us to the next handful of online fairy dust: Auto-responder follow-up systems!

Not Optional: Setting up follow-up systems so that you know a lead will be called or emailed or sms messaged or in some way communicated with were they speak to you within five minutes of them entering their information into a form.

We live in the short attention span era and your *system must have a stable, reliable follow-up system on autopilot.*

When you can get back to them within 2 minutes you turn a warm lead into a "very warm" lead; you know they saw a solution to their problem on your website, you know they need what you have, and you know there is a 90% chance you hold the solution to Mr. or Ms. Searchers problem.

This is a very warm lead, and much more likely to buy something than someone who just threw your mailer or door hanger into the trash!

TOOLBOX ALERT: There is a state-of-the-art automated follow-up software system in place that does all of this. Instant Customer fully integrates with Constant Contact, Infusionsoft, SurveyMonkey, Aweber, SalesForce, and hundreds of other applications seamlessly within a cloud based environment. When a campaign is set up correctly inside of this automated system it is predictive. Your prospective client has found you using the content creation and submission system I have been outlining so far.

Now when they are delivered into your Contact Management system (your list) will ask them questions and lead them to make a buying decision in a highly targeted manner. If they want a two bedroom condo they are sent to a list that delivers every two bedroom house in the zip codes they are looking to buy a condo in.

If they want a three bedroom house and they have a max budget of $500,000 they get a list of every house under $501,000 in the region they live or zip they specify they want to live in. They ARE NOT SENT a list that they aren't interested in, only a list of what they ARE LOOKING FOR.

Additionally there exist services that provide pre-written series of email message templates that have proven to help convert email prospects into clients. This is an excellent way to go, but you must review and edit the content and make sure to put the call to action on the right-hand side before it is submitted.

Auto-responder systems are the other piece of being oracular in your marketing system. We will thoroughly examine the follow-up process later. Now, however, it's time to get to the heart and soul of this book— being prescient, setting up intuitive systems that incorporate your website into a strategic online marketing platform that allow your prospects to find you when they look for what you sell so the search engines can send people to your site!

THE PLAIN TRUTH IS:

- Don't lose focus when designing a website: a website is for one purpose and one purpose only, and that's to get people to get in touch with you!

- Fancy is never better: plain is best here! Avoid whiz-bang Flash sites, and get a good designer to make a clean, simple, functional web site to convert leads.

-Blogs are a vital part of a website's success: make yours the home page, or at least featured prominently on the home page!

- Following up is absolutely critical: you should have automated systems in place that follow-up with your customers the moment they get in touch with you.

BONUS #MANDATORYPAGES

Text your email + #MANDATORYPAGES to (619) 722-3263 and text to receive the copy and tutorial video

3 YOUR CAMPAIGN STARTS WITH THE RIGHT KEYWORDS

If a tree falls in the woods and nobody is there... Get the idea? If you build it they will come is a losing proposition on the internet.

Having a website is necessary and it is a place you can point people to from your videos, blog posts and social network posts. It reminds me of one of the reasons I knew I could quit real estate and go to marketing online in 2002, at the time brokers would advertise their website on the Yellow Pages, and car dealers would run full page ads in the newspaper to advertise their website.

These old school brokers and dealers would spend thousands of dollars on shiny, flashy websites and spend 10s of thousands of dollars every year to show off how internet savvy they were.

You will not make that mistake because you are reading this book. The website those brokers and dealers thought they were supposed to be advertising, was actually the advertising mechanism they could have used to get exponentially more leads and sales on a tenth the money they were spending on the Yellow Pages and the local newspaper.

Those businesses that recognized their website and online marketing efforts would be the ONLY advertising they would need, invested their time and efforts into building an online platform, and build on it every day, have flourished. The bottom line is that nothing has changed.

If you have a website that no one sees then you might as well turn out the lights and go home. But not to worry, we'll get Google to notice you and rank you highly, and we'll do this using targeted keywords.

We aren't going to make this a complicated discussion, but it is an important concept to understand.

What are keywords, you ask? Keywords are the words (either one word or multiple words) that users type into Google before they click search. A multiple-word keyword, like "Chiropractor" or "Back Pain Treatment", is called a long-tail keyword phrase. When a user enters one of these keyword phrases, they will get back what Google thinks is most relevant to their search; more specifically, Google returns what it thinks are the best search results for the specific keyword phrase that the user entered in the search box.

That, in a nutshell, is what a keyword is. Our questions, however, are a tad more complicated: What keywords should we use?

What keywords will get Google to notice that we're the best search result for a specific keyword phrase?

We have many businesses who choose to have us do all of their Internet marketing for them. When we sit down at the table to discuss our plans for their Internet marketing strategies, there are two mistakes we see almost every time when we start talking about keywords:

1) Our new client will be very excited to show us that they're ranking #1 for their particular business name, like "Mesa Arizona Chiropractor". So excited, in fact, that it's almost tough to tell them that that's nothing to be excited about: next to nobody is searching for their exact company name on the Internet.

If they are, it means they already know the company and know what the company does. They've probably been reached already by one of your other marketing techniques, and you shouldn't be wasting any time on them. Not to mention that Google and the other search engines do a pretty good job of making sure that your website is going to rank high on your business name by people who search within 25 miles of your location.

Never forget: you're using the Internet to get new customers who are trying to solve a problem that you and your business can solve; in short, you need to present an attractive solution to people with problems. People need help with "back pain treatment", "cervical traction", "pain relief advice", or "lumbar relief"; these are the keywords people are putting into the search box!

Nobody's looking for "Jones, Smith, and Johnson LLC", they're looking for "lower back pain treatment" or "cervical traction in Mesa AZ", things that a chiropractor can provide a solution for. You want to rank for these keywords, and not for your business name!

2) The other big mistake we see made all the time is businesses ranking in terms that only make sense to someone who works in that particular industry.

One of the ones we've seen very frequently lately is the keyword phrase "Elder Care Law". Not many people know that elder law is an entire part of the law industry, and though they might learn about this term and start searching for that term in the future they're not doing so in great numbers right now (Google provides data about what people are searching on and while sometimes confusing to interpret -- it is free). What the ideal Elder Care Law prospect is typing in is "How can I afford long-term care", "How can I afford the nursing home", "How can I get veteran's benefits" or even "estate planning". People may not understand the terminology "Elder Care" but they do have a general idea that estate planning might be what they're trying to look for; what they're really looking for is someone to help with their parents' VA benefits or Medicaid.

The most important thing to remember in keyword selection is this: you must look at keywords from the user's perspective. You can't expect them to search for the terms you believe they're going to be able to define.

For example, don't ever go to your industry association definitions for keywords—unless, of course, it's to see which keywords not to use! It's a trap that many people fall into all the time, and you've got to watch out for it. Even we're not immune to it—we deal heavily in search and social media Internet marketing, and when we're not careful sometimes we find ourselves using terms people wouldn't use and don't care about: SEO, social media measurement.

These are things our clients would never type in! They would type in something like "I want to get more customers" instead, and so those are the keywords we really care about.

These are the two big pitfalls that we see with most businesses that we work with, and they both stem from one thing: A lack of knowledge.

Specifically, the knowledge of what people are searching for. There are a number of tools that exist out there in addition to the free Google tools, but they are changing all the time.

These various online tools are helpful, and clients who know how to use them will really benefit from the services they provide; the best (and fastest) way, however, to find the right keywords is just to ask your family and friends.

Think back to the first chapter, when we said that it's ordinary people that are using Google; that's as true for keyword usage as it is for research methods. Ask your friends, colleagues, and neighbors for help. Ask people who know you to explain to a friend what you do and ask to listen in.

They will use plain English terms to describe your business, and those are the terms that ordinary people are going to pop into that search box. The reason this works is because it gets into the mind of a client. If you gave a 60-second description of what you do to a client, and then they turn around and tell that to a friend, it's not going to sound the same—in fact, odds are it'll be very different indeed! What you're looking for in keyword selection is not how you describe your business, it's how clients and prospects describe it.

If you're not ranking on the keywords that people are searching for, nobody's going to find you.

This might be a little overwhelming, but don't worry, we're not saying that you have to nail this on the first try and you can't change keywords over time. It's not the end of the world if you choose the wrong keyword on Day 1; keywords can be modified, refined, or even completely switched out altogether.

Don't overthink your keyword selection to the point that you freeze; start off by asking your neighbors and friends, as we described above. This is a very good method to finding keywords initially, and as you get more advanced you can start using some of the tools we talked about above to refine your keyword selection. Those tools will definitely benefit, but they're not crucial right out of the gate. Start simply, as described above, and slowly grow in complexity as you master each step of the process.

Another way we use internally to refine keyword selection even further, is to use Google's "Related Searches" tool.

This will give you an idea of what others are searching for when they search for your keywords, potentially giving you an insight into related terms that you may not have thought of.

Another important tool in your keyword research arsenal is the Google Keyword Tool (GKT for short). the GKT is important because although the Related Searches tool gives you suggestions, the GKT gives you returns for how many people per month are actually searching for that keyword. This is across the entire US, so you're going to have to make an educated (and usually valid) assumption that those will work in your locality very similarly to the way they work nationally. To stick to our earlier example, let's type in two terms: "lower back pain" and "chiropractor".

You'll notice in the screenshot above that "pain relief" gets almost three times as many searches as "pain treatment". In fact, "pain treatment" is small enough that you may not even want to initially target it.

You can assume that in your locality these numbers will probably translate fairly well. It's not a given, and there's not a great tool right now for pinpointing exact numbers of local searches, but you need to assume that the national numbers will, more or less, apply reasonably well to your local searches.

If you really want a good idea of how many local searches those national numbers signify, you can do a rough calculation: take the last census date for the total US population and take the census of your location. Divide your location by the total population and it'll give you a rough estimate of the percentage of total population- multiply that times the keywords to get your number.

For example: Let's say you live in a city with one million people. The US has 300 million, by last count, which means your city has 1/300th of the amount of searches. "lower back pain treatment" returns 300k hits per month, so we can assume that your locale's getting about 1000 searches per month on that keyword. It's not exact, but it's a very good guesstimate and is often more spot-on than you'd expect!

NOTE:

Do not think that bigger is always better! Sometimes, it's better to go after an easily-dominated keyword.

The other pitfall that companies make is they typically want a neat, catchy name or their business name in the URL. If you want to rank really well, you're going to have to make your URL keyword rich.

Here's an example: Let's say you're a Chiropractor in Mesa, Arizona and you've decided on the keyword phrase " chiropractor Mesa AZ ". A great URL for your website, then, would be "http://www. chiropractorMesaAZ.com". That's going to help tremendously in your efforts to rank high on Google.

We realize that that's not a pretty name, and if you want to have your business name website URL for business cards and marketing materials you still can.

It's both inexpensive to have multiple domain names, and you can quickly have your webmaster redirect "http://www.johnsonandsmithllc.com" to "http://www.chiropractorMesaAZ.com" and still reap the benefits of the keyword-rich URL while having a professional URL on your business cards.

A keyword-rich URL is one of the first things you can do to influence your Google search rankings.

We'll talk about other methods to rocket you to the top, of course, but if you start this process without a keyword-rich URL, it's going to be a very steep uphill battle. Do yourself a favor and start with a keyword-rich URL- it's very helpful and makes everything down the line much, much easier!

Niching

With this knowledge comes another facet of Internet marketing you need to know about: niching.

As you may have guessed from that specific URL, you can't be highly ranked in everything. Unless you're a business is in a small town, there's going to be a ton of other companies vying for that top spot in many different keywords and you're going to want to select some specialty or niche to focus on.

This isn't to say that you can't do other things or cross-sell once you get your client, but you definitely have to step back and do some business strategy when it comes to niching. Where is most of your revenue coming from? Where do you want it to come from? What's your most profitable set of business? Some things require a significant amount of time, while there are other things that can just review while paralegals do most of the actual work: the second is often more profitable.

What it comes down to is this: To dominate online, you have to know where you want to go and focus on one thing. Find something that you'd be happy with if 95% of your business came from that one thing. It's there that you're going to want to start in regards to your keywords.

Dominating the search rankings under multiple keyword phrases all at once takes. Start with the most important one, the one where you want to go: it might not be where you started, but it has to be where you want to go—the niche that you want to dominate in the future.

Dominating that one keyword phrase means owning that particular source of business in your town and then you constantly build on it.

In keeping with our earlier elder care example: let's say you want to dominate the keyword "veteran's benefits". You'd make a keyword-rich URL out of that keyword-rich phrase, and then proceed to dominate the search rankings with your carefully crafted process, honed razor-sharp to focus on that particular niche.

Once you've narrowed down between 3-5 keyword phrases with a few words in them each, you'll want to make sure those keyword phrases are in your title tag in your website and that title tag starts ALWAYS with those keywords.

You want the title tag to start with the keywords, move into the location, and end with the business name. Don't lead with your business name- the business name will come along for the ride. It's all over your website, and people (and Google) aren't going to miss it.

Start instead with the important keywords, and make sure those are peppered all throughout your site.

WARNING

Don't overdo it! Google is looking for real people with real content, and not automatons who simply spew out keywords nonstop. There's a joke in the Search Engine Optimization world about this:

Q: How many Search Engine experts does it take to change a light bulb?

A: Light. Bulb. Lamp. Fluorescent. Incandescent. LED, Flashlight...

The joke is light-hearted, but the message is clear: don't over-saturate! Make sure your keywords hover around 4% density in the page text, which is the optimal percentage for keywords to words. (OK, we said we wouldn't try to confuse you about terms like keyword density and we just brought it up... we apologize, though you now know the specific data if you choose to use it.

However, stick with talking about your subject in a natural way and this will just work itself out.)

Another very, very important thing to think about in this strategy is whether or not you're in an area where someone else is already dominating that larger keyword phrase. If someone's dominating the keyword phrase you want, you have to focus on smaller subsets of that keyword phrase: if you can dominate 2 or 3 smaller keyword phrases, you may end up actually getting more business than the company that just went after that larger, broader term.

Those are, in effect, the two separate strategies you have to look at from an inside perspective. Everything in this book is important to understand for any business, because it makes you more knowledgeable. It enables you to do it yourself, or be savvy when you hire a business to do it for you. If you hire an outside business, you'll be able to make sure it's not just a webmaster that puts up a quick website but somebody who will ask these tough questions and really help you to think through the right online strategy for you. Just like the duplicate content we mentioned in Chapter One, there are lots of people just trying to sell something quick and dirty instead of doing things the right way—don't get fooled, and don't go into any negotiations without knowing what your marketing business should provide you.

Once you've got your keywords, your domain name, and your website ready, it's time to step up your game. Now, we're going to get into blogging to get ranked as well as more advanced local search techniques!

JUST THE FACTS

- Keywords are important; don't bother with trying to rank for your business name. Rank with keywords that get traffic and are terms that ordinary users are searching for!

- Incorporate your keywords into your website, and have a webmaster forward a professional-looking URL to the keyword rich one!

- Specialize, specialize, and specialize: don't go for the broad market. Find your niche or specialty and aim towards that!

- Leverage your marketing tools, especially the people around you: they are, for the most part, representative of your clients and can offer insight into how your clients would search for you.

- Be natural! Google and Bing don't like keyword stuffing; don't ever go over 4% keyword densities. Just write naturally and almost always you'll have a good amount of keyword density with a natural reading flow.

BONUS #GMAIL

Text your email + #GMAIL to (619) 722-3263 and text to receive the tutorial video showing you how to use Google's keyword tool to select keyword phrases and create a Gmail account for your business.

4 LOCALIZE YOUR MARKETING: BLOGGING & ADVANCED LOCAL SEARCH STRATEGIES

If you've been following this guide thus far, you've got a pretty reasonable setup going.

In fact, you're probably better off than anybody who just threw up a website to have an Internet presence, and you're definitely better off than anyone who has refused the transition to web-based marketing.

You may even have pulled a lead or two just from having the website, and you're considering putting your Google Places / Google + Local page up right away and watch your site skyrocket to the top of those local search returns!

We like your style, but hold on to your seat—your site's still small-fry! In this chapter, we're going to figure out how to make your local business big-time on the web using some more advanced local search techniques!

Blogging

Google has said emphatically that they're going to give stronger credit to resources that are both relevant to the user and current. This makes sense, given the overall makeup of the Internet: new content ages quickly, and very often newer info is far more useful to a person searching than old info. This problem is usually dealt with by adding new content to static web pages, but this method is time-consuming and more trouble than it's worth. Our solution? Blogging.

It is true that blogging has become the online activity-du-jour on the Internet—it seems that everyone and their cat has one, and sometimes several.

The fact of the matter is, however, that blogging has become a powerful force on the Internet; it also has one distinct advantage for us in that it's by far the easiest, most convenient, and most effective way to add new, updated content to your website. You don't have to go in and change copy all the time, you don't have to deal with static pages, HTML, and minor edits, you just have to update your blog every now and then.

It's especially helpful when you consider Google's other preference in high-ranking Google search results: steady, relevant content.

There is no "magic bullet" or fast-track way to get to the top of the Google search rankings; in this case, slow and steady wins the race. Blogging is absolutely, positively 100% all about this; it's essentially a vehicle to allow you to easily make regular, useful updates to keep your site both relevant and full of a steady stream of content.

To that end, there is a minimum amount of blog posts you should be putting out each week.

Because of Google's preference for updated, steady content, you should be blogging at the very least once per week, and each blog post should be between about 250-800 words; they can be longer but they don't need to be, and they definitely shouldn't be any shorter than 250 words or Google may mark them down as non-useful.

This may seem daunting to many, and understandably so; the thought of composing another written piece every week isn't appealing to many folks out there. If you truly think about it, however, once a week isn't too bad; that's only four times a month, and if you make a schedule and stick to it you'll find that blogging really isn't the chore you thought it would be.

If you're finding that you have time for more, it's beneficial to up your blog posts to twice a week; that's the optimal number in this sort of situation, and it'll most likely net you the most positive credit when Google compiles its local search returns. Twice a week, however, is plenty; don't go over that! Some people come into this with a very linear mindset.

They think that since 2 is better than 1, 5 must be better than 2.

It's not, and you'll experience a very diminished rate of return in

this regard; 2 blog posts a week is much better than 1, but 5

blog posts a week is barely better than 2. Bottom line is this: If

you're spending more than 2 times a week blogging, there are

other, better things you could be doing with that time!

Blog Subjects

Having a blog is all well and good, but a blog without useful,

relevant content is hardly a blog at all!

To that end, you're going to need to fill your blog with useful,

quality content that maximizes the amount of utility Google

perceives in your site. Here are the three main content points

you should be hitting in your blog posts:

1) Talk About What You Do

This one may seem pretty obvious, but it's worth mentioning:

talk about what you do, not who you are.

Don't talk about yourself, how long your business's been around, how great your service is; this isn't going to help you any. You need to fill your blog posts with quality content that relate to the services you do, quality content is valuable or useful to the user. For example, let's say you're a Realtor involved in VA benefits for helping veterans buy a home and a new law or change happened in VA benefits regulation. A perfect blog post would be a post covering these changes or relevant info pertaining to them; you could title it "VA home loan benefits answers you need to know" and phrase it as an easygoing, inside look at how the VA benefits have changed and what that could mean for anyone looking to act on them.

2) Plugged in: Talk About Local Events

#1 on this list may seem obvious to most, but this trick isn't: of all of them, this is the super-ninja secret of Internet marketing! The trick is this: talk about local events!

Blogging about things going on and tying them back into what you do is a great, great way to make Google take notice and gain credit with them in the local search return results. A good example of this would be if you lived in a city and there's a big event; talk about the big event and how it related to your community.

Let's say you live in a college town and every Saturday during football season the town quadruples in size. It's an event that polarizes many a college town- local residents are, in general, proud / frustrated about the big event, think it's good / bad for business? Think the traffic isn't worth the amount of money the game brings into the town? Do you have suggestions for parking or must hit restaurants or activities for the in-bound football fans?

You can write a blog post about this, and it'll help you with Google because Google will see that you're a part of the community and (more importantly) the blog posts gives Google lots of keyword clues about your location, really helping you to rise to the top in your location!

Additionally, don't feel pressured to make the blog post about legal issues in the community. In fact, shy away from it- these local community posts are as valuable in their own way as the legal posts you make, and someone who searches you will have plenty of time browsing your site and blog to see your other posts and find out about what you do and how you do it. This helps your business come out on top in the location it's in, because of the connection and keyword clues mentioned above; if somebody searches for "VA benefits Dallas TX" you'll show up because both your blog posts and your location-based (Dallas, TX), community-based blog posts as well.   Many, many people don't do this, and that's understandable; on the surface, it doesn't make sense to talk about things that aren't related to what you do.

TIP: You can always refer to yourself with your keywords! Don't overdo it, but it's perfectly fine to use things like "As a veterinarian in Mesa Arizona, I'm always surprised when..." . That's the best of both worlds!

Another great tip is to be proactive- go to a local newspaper site, see what they're covering, and link back to the newspaper site and talk about it. It's easy research!

This also has the added advantage of making you seem more likeable and down-to-earth, which is always a huge bonus in client interaction. When someone finds your blog and reads through it, it'll be enjoyable- she'll be getting not just practical legal advice but also feel some connection to you as well. When she reads your blog, she won't see just another faceless b- she'll read your blog posts about the community and think "Gee, this person has personality. They seem to really know what they are talking about, AND they are also a part of my community and seem really invested in it."

That person is more likely to pick up the phone and give you a call, and you just got a warm lead by being a personable blogger who talks about the community!

3) Be Natural

This ties into the last point—be natural! You don't always have to sound like the smartest person in the world on your blog. This isn't to say you should be sloppy or stupid, but you shouldn't sound like a king preaching from atop the ivory tower either. Your clients (and Google) like to see content and blog posts that appear and are from normal people. Conversation, stories, and anecdotes are all things they like to index; conversing on your blog makes you more reachable and more indexable.

This isn't just a Google-specific tactic, either; your clients will love you for it as well, as we mentioned above. It's always been a general marketing strategy to be likeable; it's the age-old marketing concept that people are more likely to work with those similar to themselves. They see your blog posts and say "Hey! This person knows what they're talking about and likes what I like." They see a real person, with a real family, and it makes them feel more comfortable working with you. A blog is the best place to do this, so plan out your blog structure accordingly. You don't have to do 52 weeks of straight specialty posting; you can do an every now and then informal, "hey, somebody asked me about this the other day and I thought I'd talk about it" post.

A good rule of thumb, if you're doing the minimum 4 times a month, is to split it up half and half: twice a month goes to business posts, and twice a month goes to local, personal stories. People like to know people, it's a fact of interaction; it will greatly help your sales when they feel that they know you more personally. This tactic may feel a little too touchy-feely for some, but don't knock it: it works very well, and blogging is a great way to do it! It drives clients and will improve your ranking, which is of course a major goal of this book.

What you should really take home from this chapter is not to underestimate the power of the local connection. We've had clients that have followed this process to the letter, and their specialty posts only gained a few hits and comments.

It was their local stories and blog posts, however, which became a focal point. conversations about how bad traffic was when a big event happened got tons of links, comments, and opinions from across the board.

In the end, this is what you want: it's the reason for this section and the reason you're branching out into the community. Not only does this sort of activity tied into your locality keywords mean big index boosts from Google, it also means very effective general marketing: it makes you a real person that people feel comfortable calling, one of the best advantages you can have in our modern, very skeptical era!

JUST THE FACTS

* Blogging is key to the success of your marketing campaign: make sure to blog at least once a week with a post that is between 250 and 800 words. If possible, blog twice a week; this is the optimal number, and blogging more than twice a week won't help you more.

* You don't have to make every blog about selling your product or service; you should alternate them between your business, product or service and events in the community.

* Be natural; this will help you be more accessible to your clients, and thus garner more page views and attention from people looking to comment on the blog as well as make you more viewable and indexable by search engines.

BONUS #HTML

Text your email + #HTML to (619) 722-3263 and text to receive two videos showing you how to use simple but necessary html code to quickly amend links in blog posts or add clickable links to an image.

5 SOCIAL SITES: THE LEGS OF YOUR PLATFORM, SOCIALCASTING TO FACEBOOK, LINKEDIN, AND TWITTER

We know some of you are skeptical. I know some of you are sitting in your home or offices, having read the title of this particular chapter, and are thinking "Twitter! Forget it, I'm not a tweeter."

Whether or not you use Twitter or Facebook or Pinterest is irrelevant, your customers are most likely using one or more of these channels to look for what you sell. As much as it pains us to say, Twitter may be one of the more important factors that figures into your Internet marketing strategy. So you better get tweeting!

Why Social Media?

Simply put: Social media is the most powerful force in how Google is determining what is relevant online.

Not only that as I write this online advertising spend has exceeded traditional broadcast advertising spend and FaceBook, LinkedIn, Twitter and other social networking sites including Google's YouTube and Google+ are part of this monumental shift in how you must advertise online to be relevant.

And, unfortunately, the online marketplace is loaded with bots, scammers, and article spinners, and many links out there are links to irrelevant or otherwise spammy articles. Social media, however, does the vetting by itself: Users of social media sites aren't going to share spammy links with each other, they're going to share real content. As a result, Google has realized that indexing and calculating relevancy from social media is very beneficial, since social media (in general) has real people posting real content, content that was valuable enough to warrant a "hey, check this out" from one person to another.

Some of us have been trying to avoid social media for one reason or the other; privacy, general lack of interest, or whatever other reason you may have avoided it thus far.

The statistics on social media and Internet marketing, however, can't be denied: for example, By 2010 Gen Y will outnumber Baby Boomers....96% of them have joined a social network.

These are the people that look and by ignoring the social media segment you're basically ignoring their primary mode of access.

* the average time on Google is three minutes. The average time on Facebook is thirteen minutes.

* Facebook, as of this writing, has over 1.11 billion users.

To put that into perspective, that means Facebook has more users than the US population; this is very important in terms of saturation. What these statistics should show you is that social media is a very, very powerful force in today's cultural mindset, and it's only getting stronger.

Social media is here to stay, and more and more people every day are joining it and receiving advice from their friends and family about great stories or services that they received.

Google has been taking notice of that and responding accordingly, and so should you. In this chapter, we're going to take a look at social networks and your strategy for them: we're going to figure how just to approach these social media websites and use them to help Google notice you!

The Social Networks

In the social media game, there are currently three huge players that we're going to focus on: Facebook, Twitter, and LinkedIn. This isn't to say you should ignore the other social media networks out there; they're still important, and in fact location-based social media like Foursquare and Facebook Places are very useful too. You may want to have a presence in those, and other minor social networks as well, like YouTube, Google+, etc.

For the core of our marketing strategy, however, we're going to focus on the big three. This focus will give you the most coverage and best ROI in terms of time spent on marketing, and so it's how we'll proceed!

Facebook

Facebook is the biggest social media site in the world, the 800-pound gorilla online; everybody knows and uses it, so you're going to need to capitalize on that. The first thing you should have is a fan page, and so we'll take a look at how to create one and how to link it into your overall Internet marketing strategy.

TIP:

Many of you will be scared of Facebook's privacy implications. It's very important to note that your business fan page is NOT your personal page. It's not connected to your personal page, it's not the same thing as your personal page, and nothing you post on your personal page will appear on your business page or vice versa. They are completely separate entities! For those you of you resisting joining Facebook / are afraid your fan page will expose your personal page, fear not: none of your personal information will go on your fan page, and your privacy is safe.

Your Facebook Fan Page

A fan page, quite simply, represents your business. Facebook fan pages can have dynamic pages that offer info about your business- first you need an opt-in box on the page, a custom iframe is the way to do this as of the writing of this book. This is code placed on the landing page for your fan page; your web developer or webmaster should be able to do this pretty easily. When new visitors come to the fan page they will see the information in the iframe, which will be an opt-in box and benefit information; this will be very similar to the calls to action you have on your main website- "3 things to know before you call a veterinarian", that sort of thing.

The great part of this fan page is that you're adding new clients onto an email marketing list through a social media channel. It's a very organic way of getting warm leads and targeted marketing. These people are already in the social media world, surfing around, and in their social network traversal they stumble on your fan page and think "Wow! I might need a veterinarian for my Pomeranian". In fact, the #1 growing demographic of Facebook is 25-34 and 35-54 year old females

This is a massive, growing target market for many, many people who need veterinarian for all kinds of pets. It's definitely the right mix of people with the money and the motive to hire veterinarian, and your fan page on Facebook will be a great place for them to get in touch with you regarding their problems. While you're creating your Facebook fan page, don't forget about your Facebook Places page as well. The location-based aspect of this is really attractive, especially because of the proliferation of mobile phones. More and more people are buying smartphones and more and more things are going mobile; with a Places page, people can check in and see what's around them, and you can offer specials through this mode of delivery.

At least get on this radar, but you can take it further- be

creative! Combine things like your Fan page and Places page, and figure out ways to synergize the two to make an effective marketing vehicle!

This is perhaps the most important thing to know about social media in general; all of these things can be linked together in different ways. There are so many options for managing Fan pages and Places pages that it's vital you have a professional who knows how to set up social media correctly. Barring that, you need to get online and do some extensive research into establishing the proper social media channels; it's not something you can just cobble together quickly.

Once you've got your Fan page and Places set up, it's time to

move on!

Twitter

Twitter—one of the newest social networks out there, and perhaps one that inspires the most reluctance to join. It's been much vilified by the media and our peers, but the fact remains that Twitter is important:

it's the most open social network out there.

In fact, this is the whole reason Twitter is so important. Every single tweet (a "tweet" is what each individual Twitter post is called) is indexed by Google. Other social networks, like Facebook and LinkedIn, need a username and password to see most of their content; with Twitter, there's no requirement to log in to see individual tweets.

What this means is that Google can index all the tweets out there, and this means that Twitter informs Google page rankings enormously; Google is using people's tweets to help gauge the importance of pages all around the Internet. Pages with lots of links from Twitter, for example, are going to increase its importance: you don't want to be spammy, but you do want to take advantage of this fact.

That's the basis of most of your Twitter interaction, when it's all said and done: taking advantage of Twitter's ability to generate constant content without coming across as being spammy.

You can't just blast out links to your blog articles all day; a stream of useless / irrelevant content from you (or rehashed content) isn't going to help you to increase your page rank.

Much like the techniques described in "Go Local Big-time", you're going to want to create a bunch of tweets about local things like events as well as topical content like minor changes, changes that would be important or useful for people to know. Your tweets are going to be composed of similar content to your blogs, except shortened down to the 140 character limit per tweet, and sent out once or twice a day.

This may seem as daunting as the blogging, especially considering the daily frequency of the tweets. Truth be told, however, 140 characters is not that much at all, and you don't have to sit by the computer and send them out one by one; there are tons of websites / programs that let you schedule tweets, including HootSuite (http://hootsuite.com), SocialOomph (http://www.socialoomph.com), and more. You can sit down for an hour and write enough tweets for a week or two, schedule them, and forget about them until the next week

when you sit down to write some more!

Don't be tempted just to tweet an exact duplicate of your blog

posts or articles!

Your tweets should be on the same content as your blog posts,

but they shouldn't be copied and pasted straight from the blog.

What you can do, however, is to link back to your blog from

your tweets: in fact, this is not only permissible but encouraged!

There are many, many plugins for countless blogging platforms that enable you to automatically send out a tweet with a link to your blog post every time you post a new blog post. Take advantage of that to generate links to your blog posts—that's not spammy since it's only once or twice a week, and it's a great tool for slowly and steadily creating links back to your blog. There are also plugins for Facebook as well—make sure when you post a blog, it's getting automatically posted to your Twitter and Facebook page!

LinkedIn

In the social media circles, LinkedIn is often completely overshadowed by its bigger social media cousins Facebook and Twitter. It is instead regarded as just a professional or resume-sharing site and nothing more; this is a big misstep for many, as LinkedIn is an enormous cash cow if used properly.

For starters, LinkedIn itself is no slouch in terms of financial recognition; now publicly traded (LNKD), Linked In has a market cap of $8-$10 billion (or $70-$100 per user)—making it a very formidable, fast-growing contender in the social media sphere.

Additionally, LinkedIn has an added attraction to us that isn't related to its market share. Because of LinkedIn's status as a site for professionals and resume-swapping, the average LinkedIn user is far more likely to be a potential client because of the means / motive aspect we described earlier with Facebook.

1. Over one fifth of users are Middle Management level or above

2. Almost 60% have a College or Post Grad degree

3. Average Household Income is $88,573.

4. All of these numbers are higher than published statistics for Wall Street Journal, Forbes, or BusinessWeek.

Put simply, LinkedIn users are wealthier and have more need for services and non-useful demographics, like teenagers, aren't crowding the LinkedIn user space to post pictures of their friends and pets. LinkedIn is composed of your potential clients interacting with each other, looking for professionals and just waiting to be introduced to your business.

Press Releases

This isn't really social media, but we're going to incorporate it into this section because it deals with controlling a message that goes out and can get shared and receive comments; in a sense, the medium of the Internet itself is social. PR is also one of the few places where Google expects duplicate content; the more duplicated/shared the press release is, the more important the content must be.

15 Great Press Release Ideas:

1. **Someone in your company is speaking at an industry conference, local chamber, rotary club, etc.**

2. **You hire someone new into your company**

3. **Someone is promoted**

4. **You join an association (local or national)**

5. **You start offering a new service or product**

6. **New office space or additional office added**

7. Successful client -- create a Case Study and send out press release

8. Awards received or recognition from local or national industry or association

9. Employee or officers named to charity benefit or non-profit board

10. Large sponsor of a charity benefit

11. New Business contract awarded

12. Having a big promotion or sweepstakes or contest - issue a press release

13. Your product and services tie into a big current event news item (new government law, health discovery, tax time, new hot-topic movie release, etc.)

14. Launch of a new website (hint, hint)

15. The release of your special report (hint hint)

There are both paid and free press sites out there; the paid press sites are worth the money sometimes because they go out to Associated Press and other big name news wires, like Yahoo and Google News. The more that your story gets out there, the more possibility it is that it could get picked up; a local paper could see that press release and pick up the story, for example, and that's a great thing to take advantage of. The problem of duplicate content goes out the window because duplicate content is expected in press releases, and often the big names, like Associated Press and Reuters, even source duplicate content!

GOOGLE+:

What makes Google+ different from Facebook, LinkedIn, YouTube and Twitter?

This is not Google's 1st attempt at social. There are many social networks, but let's focus on the big 4 Facebook, LinkedIn,

YouTube and Twitter. Understanding how these sites operate

helps explain Google+

YouTube – I make a video. You search for it and can watch,

share, or comment on my video. As a search based network

this is the most open network of them all. Few people use the

subscribe function as a social element.

Linkedin – Use to be: Here is my resume please hire me — Now

is: I need a job, I collaborate with my colleagues & vendors to

learn and grown in groups, and I get / answer questions.

The most closed network of the 4, you must know my email,

already have worked with me, or be in a group with me to

connect.

Twitter – I can push information out to many people and this

information can be spread quickly. Google indexes this

network, which is a bonus. As many people as are on Twitter

can follow my updates. You can follow me and I do not need to

follow you.

Information is sent out in short burst and interaction takes place both on Twitter (in a short conversation style) and off Twitter (follow this link to see this video, read my blog, etc.)

Facebook - The current king of social media. Facebook is about "friendships". You and I must mutually like each other to share information. I can post information with hopes that this information is seen on your News Feed.

There is no guarantee my information will be seen by my friends. Facebook controls information and uses an algorithm called Edge to determine what information they believe I want to see. There is a great business component with Pages (formally fan pages).

Google+ What makes you so different?

From a big picture Google+ is all about connecting all of your computer uses both online and offline in one place. We are talking cloud on a major scale.

We are talking about your documents, spreadsheets, applications, videos, everything being available in one location and everything being one click from something you can share.

This brings us to the MAJOR DIFFERENCE of Google+

So this is great, I can share all my information from my blog to my expense report, but I don't want to share everything with the world. My mom does not need to know about everything about work and my clients don't want to know about my personal life. Google+ plus has created a revolutionary function called CIRCLES. Circles control both the stream of information out and in. People you connect with are organized into different circles.

How do Circles work and why are they important?

1) You can create any circle you want. Examples of my circles include: Following, Friends, Best Friends, Employees, Clients, Vendors, Very Smart Marketing People, Fellow Online Marketers, Funny Peeps, Family

2) The people you connect with can be in multiple circles. Some people that are Very Smart Marketing People are also my Friends

3) I can choose to send information to one, or more, circles. This information will appear on their wall or can be sent as a message. The great thing is if I share something with my client circle only then no one else sees that post on their feed. Maybe we just got back from a family vacation and I want to share the photos with my family and friends but do not want to bother my vendors, clients, and the general public with the images.

4) I can choose to see information from one or more circles in my feed. Instead of being told what content an algorithm thinks I would like to see, I can choose my content feed based on my circles. This allows me to quickly and easily navigate from one set of feeds to the next. Since you can have people in multiple circles, I know that I am seeing what I want from whom I want.

Here are a few other features to Google+

- Multiple Video Chat. Google+ will allow you to connect with up to 10 people on live video chat at the same time. The feature is smooth and audio is good. A real great way to connect with people for virtual meetings. The best part of this feature is the person talking gets the main screen.

- Larger image and video display on the wall. When you post a video or images they are about 3 times larger on the wall when compared to Facebook.

- Easy navigation to all of Google's functions. While on Google+ you can search the web, see your Gmail messages, and access your Google Documents.

- Simple share option. This is very similar to Facebook google uses both a +1 button (similar to Facebook's like) and a "share this post" option.

- 1 click and you can add someone.

If you see a name in a post, find someone in your friends feed, or stumble upon someone of interest you can add them without navigating to their page. This is very convenient. When you hover over their name you a box appears giving you the option to add them to a circle.

Setting up Google+ is simple. Similar to other social media outlets, there is an area for information about you, pictures, website URLs, and basic data. As always, only share what you are comfortable sharing. Make sure your about me section has benefits to working with you and keywords for your industry. Like Linkedin there is a title are that you should also include keywords about your area of practice.

The difficult part about social media is that it is rapidly changing. We have created an area where you can go to get the most up-to-date information about social media and the changes to the various networks.

Press Releases are so important to the overall online strategy that we decided this year to start writing, publishing, and syndicating releases on behalf of our clients. Once again, we found that the average business owner has better things to do than write press releases all day. Maybe you have the time... our clients certainly don't. Either way, press releases have to be a part of the overall success strategy online.

With that, our foray into social media has ended; next up on our list is directory listings!

Just The Facts:

- Social media is one of the most important forces in marketing today: it can't afford to be ignored, and you need to set up strategies for dealing with it.

- The three biggest social media players right now are Facebook, Twitter, and LinkedIn: you need to have pages for them and have a system set up on your blog that pushes blog updates to the respective social networks.

- Google+, though new, is rapidly growing: make sure to incorporate it into your marketing strategy!

- Press releases are an extremely important part of your online marketing strategy, so much so that you should have your marketing business do it for you and cut down on the immense amount of time you're spending on it.

- Social media is rapidly changing, and no single strategy will stay effective forever; make sure to keep your campaigns updated to stay ahead of the game!

BONUS #FACEBOOK

Text your email + #FACEBOOK to (619) 722-3263 and text to receive a video tutorial showing you step-by-step how set up a Facebook page for your business, product or service.

6 LET YOUR CUSTOMERS FIND YOUR BUSINESS BY USING ONLINE DIRECTORIES

If you've been an Internet user since the pre-search days, you'll recognize directory listings. Directory listings are, in short, the online version of the Yellow Pages: Super Pages, YellowPages.com, Yahoo Local, Bing Places, Google Places / Google + Local, etc..

These directories are commonly called "citations" by those in the Internet marketing and search marketing industry. There are hundreds of them across the Internet; there are, however, 12-15 major ones where you want to be listed.

In addition to the main directories like MerchantCircle.com,

SuperPages.com, Yelp.com, and Yahoo Local, businesses should be sure to get listed on AVVO.com. The majority of these services allow for a free listing. You should not need anything more than that. Resist the urge and the follow-on emails and phone calls trying to upsell you into a paid option.

A paid listing or preferred listing may be right for you depending on your market, but do everything else first and after you have a baseline for your online success, test the gain in calls or emails you receive by opting for a paid enhancement to a directory listing. That way you can measure the real cost/benefit of the investment.

Some directories, like InfoUSA, are even more influential and you must be sure your information is correct and optimized there because other directories pull information from them; in time, as other directories use the information there, your information will proliferate all over the Internet. Make sure it is the right information. These directories/citations give you prominence because of Google's local search return policies, since Google has moved its local search returns to its main page, using Google Places / Google + Local. The algorithm that determines which Google Places / Google + Local business listings belong on the first page of Google search results takes a great deal of its weighting consideration by looking around the Internet to see if your business is listed elsewhere. If you're in 5, 10, or even 15 directory listings (with reviews in the local area) that's going to look very good in Google's ranking system. We'll get to reviews in the next chapter, but suffice it to say that directory listings with reviews are very helpful; if your competition is getting more reviews than you, you often won't make the first page and they will!

You're going to want to be on a great many directories; there are some services out there that will do this for you, but quite often the best way to do it is to do it manually. You really want to be in control of this—some services are pretty spotty in this regard, and they'll slip in shady techniques or insist that you stay out of the process. It's not that hard or time-consuming, and we recommend doing it manually; just go through the top 10-15 directory listings, enter in your data, put photos, and fill out the details as much as you can. Make sure to use keywords and geolocation in your description; geolocation is just an SEO term for city / state. In keeping with our previous example, if you're a Realtor and your keywords are "VA benefits", you could put in your description "VA benefits Realtor in Houston, Texas".

How to List Yourself

It's a pretty easy process to list your business, all things considered. You just have to go to these directories and their websites, and list yourself. Some are paid, but many are free and just try to upcharge you with different services once you've listed yourself on the directories. Don't about these upcharges and paid directory listings, but they're really not necessary. Our experience is that, done correctly, you never need to pay for directory listings or any of the extra services the free ones offer you; judicious and skillful use of keywords and geolocation will be more than enough to bump you up to the top.

I've had many clients top-ranked in Google Places / Google + Local who never paid for directory listings, and it's unlikely that you'll ever have to pay for a directory listing or upcharge either. That is not to say that these additional paid services won't provide more traffic and clients to your business, but don't start there.

Be ready for phone calls from those directories though, as they will be looking to sell you upcharges and service add-ons.

Changes to Google and other advertising venues online have left many of these directories rethinking their business models and scrambling by the wayside; paying for a directory listing is no longer as necessary as it used to be.

You'll have many directories telling you to upcharge this and upcharge that and pay for advertising, but don't do it: stay steadfast, keep on trucking, and you'll see that it wasn't necessary at all to pay for any services that the directory listings tried to offer you!

WARNING:

Big warning here! This is a problem that we run into with many local businesses that have partners in the same office. What happens is that often in an office, you have 3-4 commission sales agents that are really in a one office partnership; sometimes, each of them will go in and create their own listings, so you end up with multiple listings for each business entity, and one for the office as a whole.

When Google queries the directory listings, it gets confused at the multiple entries for the one address; it thinks it's an attempt to game the system and may ignore them all.

You want to go in and be very, very careful that you only have one listing; search for your address, business name, other people in the office, anything you can think of to identify multiple listings. If you do have multiple listings and didn't know it, delete them all! Get down to zero and start from scratch; it's much better that way. If for some reason you can't delete them all, at least get down to one and edit that one as best you can.

It used to be a big trick to list duplicate listings to boost search rankings, and so now Google cracks down on it very hard. Remember: duplicate listings are bad! Too many dupes, and Google completely ignores them all. Be very wary of this, and search hard for duplicate listings!

Another important thing to remember when you're doing directory listings is to make sure to use keywords and geolocation only in the short / long descriptions that the directory listings give you. Do not use keywords in your business name! This is why you have a keyword-rich URL; if the URL was the business name you'd have to use that and not get the keyword benefit. Google does not like to see business names stuffed with keywords and geolocation; that will definitely hurt you in the long run.

This can be turned to your advantage, depending on how dedicated you are to this strategy; some of our sharper clients have actually changed their business name to include keywords and geolocation, like "Elder Law of Georgia Business".

This may recall the Yellow Pages game of putting A's in business names to get to the top of the listings, like "AA Best Dentist of Dallas, Texas".

If your company name officially contains your keywords and location, Google is OK with that; what they're watching out for is obvious keyword stuffing like "Smith and Jones Realty – real estate – homes for sale - VA loan - Houston TX". That's a no-no, make sure you put those keywords in your description, NOT in your business name.

If the directory listing has suggested keywords, consider using them; it probably looks very similar to the Yellow Pages categories you are used to seeing.

Some places give you a chance to type in yours, in which case do so. Don't go crazy, however, because Google only values about 3-4 keywords; anything after that they consider gaming the system and just ignore.

Here is a list of directories that your business needs to be listed on.

1. Google Places / Google + Local

2. Yahoo!

3. YellowBot

4. Yelp

5. WhitePages

6. MapQuest

7. SuperPages

8. CitySearch

9. YellowBook

10. Local.com

11. MerchantCircle

There are about 40 more directory listings that we list our

clients on. Some of these directory listings are more relevant today than a year from now. Do some research and find at least 15 more directories to list your business on top of the core 11 above.

Google Places / Google + Local

Google Places / Google + Local, though technically a listing, deserves a special mention here. The Google Places / Google + Local listing should be the absolute last thing you should create; get the rest of the directory listings in first, wait a month or so until you have a few reviews, and then create your Google Places / Google + Local page. This wait time is very important-it's so important, in fact, that if we meet clients who already have a Google Places / Google + Local listing before this structure is in place we sometimes advise them to delete it and start over unless it's already in the top 7 listings. If it's not on the first page, delete it, do this process, and then add it a month later.

The reason behind this is that when you create a Google Places / Google + Local page, it goes forth and looks for all the info about you: Directory listings, blogs, reviews, etc. and so forth. If you've done all the things we've talked about it should help rocket way up to the top of the list once you create it; if you want to be on the first page, waiting those four weeks to make a Google Places / Google + Local listing makes a huge, huge difference in your ranking!

Also, another powerful, yet rarely discussed advertising medium is Pay Per Click advertising...the best example of which is Google AdWords. AdWords is pound-for-pound the single quickest way to get your business listed on Page #1 of Google. You can do it in 10 minutes or less. It will cost you a few dollars a day (when you know what you are doing). Or it could cost you thousands (if you don't). The key is to have your ads show ONLY in your geographical area. Our recommendation is to find someone who is skilled at AdWords and pay them to do your ads. It will pay off for you in the end.

Just The Facts:

- There are hundreds of directory listings out there; be smart and only join the 10-15 that are the biggest and most relevant (yelp, AVVO, etc.)

- You can pay people to put you on directories, but the best and cheapest way is to do it yourself. Most directories are free. They'll try to get you with up-sells and add-ons, but don't bother. They don't help.

- Don't put keywords in your business name in the directories; Google doesn't like it unless those keywords are officially part of your business name.

- You'll be tempted to put up a Google Places / Google + Local along with the directories, but don't. Since Google pulls information about you when you create the Google Places / Google + Local page, it's best to wait a month or so and create after you've gotten a few reviews.

7 DRIVE PROSPECTS TO YOUR BUSINESS WITH ONLINE REVIEWS

This part of the system really confuses some people, especially since reviews are created by clients and customers. How can reviews make or break a search engine ranking?

Sure, they might be helpful for clients talking to clients, but they surely can't influence Google's monstrous ranking machine in your favor. Can they?

As it turns out, they can and they do influence the ranking system.

Very much so, in fact; Google uses reviews in order to judge the validity of the place in question.

Put simply, if the location's been reviewed, someone's been

there, and the review comments also give an indication of the

quality of the location and whether or not it deserves to be

ranked higher or lower. Many of these reviews allow reviewers

to give star ratings, which are even more influential: Google

scrapes these numbers automatically to do a sort of website

litmus test, a judgment of whether or not the establishment is

overall positive or negative. In fact, Google has recently

adjusted the Google Places / Google + Local page user interface

to prominently display the "Write a review" button to

specifically encourage reviews within Google's own systems.

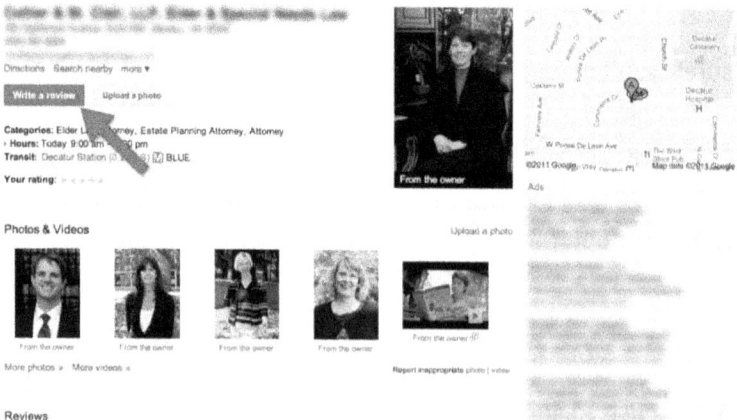

Review sites are, in general, the directory listings we talked about earlier; Google uses the info to determine whether or not you're the best solution to the problem that the user is trying to solve.

This is important- the whole idea of the ranking system and your marketing strategy is to make Google see that you are, in fact, the best solution to the problem!

Another key point to this strategy is that many of your competitors are simply not getting reviews at all.

This is especially true in the Internet marketing strategies; we've done extensive research specifically with local businesses, and very few have any reviews at all, as evidenced by this Google Places / Google + Local page here:

divorce attorney st. louis mo

About 187,000 results (0.40 seconds)

Saint Louis Divorce Lawyers, Attorney, Lawyer, Attorneys, Law ...
lawyers.findlaw.com/lawyer/firm/Divorce/Saint-Louis/Missouri - Cached
Results 1 - 20 of 44 – Find **Saint Louis Divorce Lawyers**, Attorney, Lawyer, Attorneys, Law
Firms - **MO** - **Divorce lawyers** in **Saint Louis Missouri**.

Family Law Attorney Serving Clayton, **St. Louis, Missouri** - The ...
www.thecarsonlawfirm.com/ - Cached
Leigh Joy Carson is an aggressive litigator with compassion for **family law** issues. Areas of
practice include **divorce**, child custody, mediation, visitation. ...

St. Louis County **Family Law Lawyer MO | Missouri** Divorce Law ...
www.familylawstlouis.com/ - Cached
Contact a divorce and **family law attorney** from the Law Offices of Carla J. Zolman in **St.
Louis, Missouri**. Call 866-780-9435.
(A) 2016 South Big Bend, Saint Louis
(314) 333-4153

Place page

Cynthia Fox Family Lawyers | St Louis Divorce Lawyer, Child ...
foxfamilylawyers.com/ - Cached
Focused on all aspects of family law: divorce, child custody, child support; Cynthia Fox has
been a top **divorce lawyer in St. Louis** for over 25 years. ... Attorney at law 7751 Carondelet
Avenue, Suite 700. Clayton, **Missouri** 63105 ...
(B) 7751 Carondelet Avenue, Suite 700, Saint Louis
(314) 727-4880
stltoday.com (1)

Zero Reviews

Place page

St. Louis Divorce, Mediation & **Family Law Attorney | Missouri** ...
www.consideringdivorce.com/ - Cached
Contact a top **family law attorney** in **St. Louis, Missouri**. Call the Law Office of Marta J.
Papa at 1-888-713-9308.
(C) 7101 Delmar, Saint Louis
(314) 862-0202
yahoo.com (2)

Place page

St. Louis Divorce Lawyer | St. Charles Child Custody Attorney ...
www.stangelawfirm.com/ - Cached
Family law concerns? Contact a **St. Louis divorce lawyer** at the Stange Law Firm LLC in **St.
Louis, Missouri**, by calling 314-963-4700.
(D) 1750 South Brentwood Boulevard #401, Saint Louis
(314) 963-4700

★★★★★
7 reviews
Place page

Tonya Page, **Attorney** at Law
www.stlouis-divorce.com/
February 20th, 2011 -Tonya D. Page is an **attorney** handling ... St. Louis and
throughout the state of **Missouri**. In addition to **divorce** ...
(E) 1232 Washington Avenue #220, Saint Louis
(314) 504-0584

Less than 10 Reviews

1 review
Place page

Lindhorst Law Firm
maps.google.com
(F) 1308 Papin Street, Saint Louis
(314) 241-5553

1 review
Place page

Uthoff, Graeber, Bobinette & Blanke
www.ugbblaw.com/
St Louis Business Law **Lawyer | Missouri** Personal Injury **Attorney** | University City Probate
Law Firm
(G) 906 Olive Street - Suite 300, Saint Louis
(314) 621-9550

Place page

More results near St Louis, MO »

Bankruptcy Lawyer - Real Estate Lawyer - Family Law Attorneys - Personal Injury Attorney - Criminal Attorney

Notice that these businesses have no reviews, or a low number of them! As a result, you don't need to get a billion reviews on your directory listings and Google Places / Google + Local page; you just need to have a little consistency and make sure you're getting a couple reviews a month on just 2 or 3 different directories (one of which must be Google Places / Google + Local).

To start, you're going to need to size up how many reviews you need to rank. Do some review research on your keywords; type them into Google and see how many reviews the top ranked results have. If they have five reviews, you need ten- if they have two hundred, well... you've got a lot of work to do! Typically local businesses have somewhere in the ten to twenty range when it comes to number of reviews (and many markets don't have any we have found).

For the most part, in order to beat them at the rankings game, you'll need to have about double the amount of reviews they have.

Keep in mind that these are total reviews: for example, if you need twenty reviews, you can spread it over four months. That's just five reviews per month, which is certainly doable, and we'll talk about how to get those reviews in a second.

Review Sites

First things first, however, on which sites should you be focusing on getting reviews? There are tons of them out there, and some of them don't matter and some of them do.

How do you figure out which ones are worth your time and which ones aren't?

Thankfully, there's a fairly efficient way to do it. First off, half the work is done: many of these review sites are also directory listings, and you've already listed yourself on the top directory listings. What you have to do, then, is to do a Google keyword search in your location and go through the pages at the bottom.

Don't go digging too far; you're rarely going to have to go digging down through the pages.

If you scroll down to the bottom, you'll see numbers as far as the mouse can click. For your part, you're just interested in the top 5 directories that are already listed; make a list of your directory listings and cross-reference which ones appear first in the Google keyword search. For example, if you are a Real Estate Agent in Denver Colorado, then you should google "real estate agent + your business name". Then look at the results and find the first 3-5 listings that refer to an online directory site like Yelp, CitySearch, or SuperPages. The 3-5 that appears first are the ones you're going to want to focus on.

It's also OK if you don't find 5; you may only find 2 or 3 at the beginning, and that's fine. This is normal- sometimes it can take search engines quite some time to properly index all the information out there. To give you some perspective, there are about ten thousand new websites created every day; this is a gigantic amount for search engines to index, and so often there's a lag time as the search engines crawl the pages and index them.

Your mission here is to find the ones that are ranked, and of those find the top ranked ones; these are the ones where you're going to focus your review techniques!

TIP:

If there are a great number of reviews for your keyword niche, consider focusing on one or two. If you have a competitor who has saturated your niche with reviews, Google the keyword phrases they use to find out which review sites are consistently being pulled up the most; focus all your review efforts on those review sites and use your campaign keyword sets. As an example, if your keyword is "emergency plumber Edina Minnesota" and the majority of reviews are being pulled from CitySearch, then CitySearch is the best place to start.

Getting Reviews vs Testimonials

Now that we've narrowed down our target directories, let's get reviews on them. We'll start with your current clients: it'll be easier to get reviews from them, as they're right in the middle of working with you.

It's important to note here that we understand that some businesses sometimes not allowed to ask for testimonials (attorneys in certain states for example). You need to understand this because this is important: if you are concerned about this issue then just remember to phrase the request correctly by not asking for a testimonial, but simply asking for someone to go to a website and put in a review. It's on a public forum where they could leave the review with or without your assistance. You're going to want to have a card produced, see our sample below, that you hand to your clients as they walk out the door; this card will tell them where to go and how to write a review. This is absolutely crucial!

Thank you for being a trusted client of ours. Please take a few moments to log into one of these sites and write a quick a review, this will be of great service to us.

- www.Yelp.com/EstatePlanningBoiseID.com
- www.Google.places.com/EstatePlanning BoiseID.com

If you have any questions please contact us directly 555.555.5555

Note - Here is a definition of the ranking system:
★ We completely let you down
★★ There were problems w/ our service
★★★ We could have done better
★★★★ Our services met your expectations
★★★★★ You enjoyed working w/ us

Sample Review For Your Reference:

- "The service was polite and they really made a difficult circumstance comfortable. I am so glad we went to Boise Estate Planning attorney Jane Smith..."
- "I have been working with Boise Estate Planning attorney Jane Smith for years and I am glad to have you in my corner and on my side, thanks for always getting done what you promise"
- "At first I was unsure if I needed any firm. After a few visits I am so glad I chose Boise Estate Planning attorney Jane Smith. Not only did I need a firm Jane really made the whole process painless."

WARNING:

You cannot, under any circumstances, go in to these websites and create the reviews for your clients. They also can't give you the reviews and you write the reviews; Google will know from the IP address that these reviews are all coming from the same location and they will ignore it at best and hurt your ranking or get rid of your listing altogether at the worst. This is true even if they are real reviews that clients mailed you; a common scammer trick is to have teams of people writing multiple reviews, and as such Google is searching that spam out and penalizing that harshly.

Under no circumstances should your clients write reviews from your location; they have to go to their computer at their house, business, or coffee shop and write the review there. This is vital!

This also extends to other computers in your office. There is a common setup we see fairly often; businesses will have a "review" computer set up in the office, where clients can go and enter in a review.

This falls into the same trap as the scenario above, and we always warn clients against this when we see it: Google is tracking these reviews, and even though it's not you typing, unfortunately, it's coming from the same place. Google can't distinguish these from scammers who employ that same trick, and thus having this "review station" isn't going to help you at all.

They absolutely, positively have to do it on their computer in their home or business; there's no way around this and it's very important for you to remember this!

WARNING:

Be very, very, very careful about who you hire to do your review process! There are many services out there that will solicit you and claim to be able to get you lots of reviews. Very often, these services are near-spam type businesses that just create all the reviews themselves and post them from one IP address; not only is this not going to help you, this sort of review fabrication is against the law. You have to be very careful about who you consult and how; if you talk to a company that says they'll get you twenty reviews in a week, you should be very cautious. We've even seen reviews from businesses we've worked with that have used such services; the result shows 20 reviews for different businesses that are all just the same sentence with the business name replaced.

Do not use a service! If you absolutely must, make sure you build your process with a proven agency / partner. We provide our clients with an entire review process whitepaper.

As an example of this, we have a process where we do calling /

mailers for the clients depending on their individual needs. We keep close communication with the client and have an active role due to the nature, sensitivity, and importance of reviews; this is how your service, if you use one, should treat you. Make sure the service keeps very close to your business and ultimately gives your business the ultimate control over the review process. This is a crucial part of hiring a service—don't forget it whenever you're looking around for these agencies or services.

And... since you picked up this book you likely would have an interest in having one of associates personally review your website and online strategy, go to…
www.ChannelMarketingAgency.com – this URL gives you a coupon that makes this $400 review free for you, since you are reading and implementing the things in this book. Note, while it's free, we're busy, and availability may be limited. It's a great opportunity to get your online presence reviewed by one of our experts.

The best way to get these reviews, as mentioned above, is to hand out your card. Don't stop there, however: another great way is mailing or emailing clients asking for reviews (see our sample below). Make it a team effort- insert into the email where you're ranking and where your competitors are ranking, and explain that you want to get to the top and get reviews as well.

~~~~~~

Subject:
What does ice cream and Law have in common?

Body:
There are always a million flavors to choose from, but when you find one you like you stick with it. We all have our favorite ice cream and we hope that our firm is your favorite.

We are writing you today to say hello and wish you the best. As part of our efforts to continue to provide the best service to our clients we need to ask you for a quick favor.

Take a moment and go to one of the websites below and leave us a review. This will help us improve and grow as a firm. As a loyal client we want to say thank you in advance.

To make things simple below are a few samples and here is a quick guide to the review process:
Here is a definition of the ranking system:
* We completely let you down
** There were problems w/ our service
*** We could have done better
**** Our services met your expectations
***** You enjoyed working w/ us

Visit one of these two sites:
http://www.ReviewSiteNumber1.com/yourfirm
http://www.ReviewSiteNumber2.com/yourfirm

Again, thank you.
Best Wishes,
Law Firm of LeBret Homer & Rush
http://www.EstatePlanningAttorneyNoWhereUSA.com

Sample Review For Your Reference:
* "The service was polite and they really made a difficult circumstance comfortable. I am so glad we went to Boise Estate Planning attorney Jane Smith..."
* "I have been working with Boise Estate Planning attorney Jane Smith for years and I am glad to have you in my corner and on my side, thanks for always getting done what you promise"
* "At first I was unsure if I needed any firm. After a few visits I am so glad I chose Boise Estate Planning attorney Jane Smith. Not only did I need a firm Jane really made the whole process painless."

~~~~~~

Remember that this isn't all about Google Places / Google +

Local; we want to send people to a few different directories.

You do of course want reviews going to Google Places / Google

+ Local as well, but you need to diversify: have cards with other

review sites on them as well, such as Yelp, CitySearch, and the others that you've identified in your target directory listings. Try not to put them all on one card, however: it looks cramped, awkward, and unprofessional. A card per review site looks much better, and it'll work better in getting clients to go to the review sites for you.

The same goes for your emails; your clients may already have an account on one of these review sites and then it would be even easier for them to leave a review saying what a wonderful job you did! This also helps even more since identified reviews count even more than anonymous ones!

Again, it's important to note that these are absolutely, positively not testimonials: these are things consumers can go and do on their own. In fact, you're simply trying to encourage a behavior that's already happening: don't be surprised if, when you start this process, you already have a couple of reviews scattered around the Internet. All you're doing is encouraging this process: you're saying "Hey, there are these review sites out there and having reviews help us. You might do it already, and if you liked our service, your review will really help our Internet ranking and get more people into our door!"

You'll find, more often than not, that people are more than willing to help you out in this regard! They'll go to these sites and fill out reviews, and this is super-important: it's one of the driving forces behind the Google Places / Google + Local rankings, and by having this steady system of reviews you're ensuring your steady climb to the top!

Just The Facts:

* Reviews are very important, and should not be overlooked: search the review sites and find out which ones you should be focusing on.

* Make sure you have a system in place to get users to review you: this is different from testimonials!

* Whatever you do, don't have a computer in your office for clients to write reviews (and absolutely don't write their reviews for them). Google requires the reviews to be written by the

client on a computer outside of the office, and so the reviews

need to be done on the client's own computer!

   - Be careful about who you hire to do your review marketing: some marketers will promise huge numbers but write fake reviews with duplicate content and severely damage your Google ranking!

8 AUTOMATING YOUR SYSTEM (USING APPLICATIONS TO SUBMIT CONTENT & "TALK" TO YOUR CLIENTS)

Follow-up strategies are a vital segment of any Internet marketing strategy, and it's equally vital that you automate it as much as possible; many businesses will try to do this manually, but the overhead required to manually implement isn't feasible for most businesses. It's vital that you don't spend manual time fielding emails and responding one by one; we've had clients in the past that literally sent out e-mail newsletters every week by hand. If somebody new came in, they'd get manually added to this email list.

That sort of system may work in the beginning, but it's easy to see that it doesn't scale up well at all; you need an automated method of follow-up that both preserves quality but also scales out well, freeing up resources and keeping your Internet marketing strategy running smoothly and efficiently!

Follow-up Framework

First off, we have to talk about the framework for follow-up: when we're talking about follow-up, we're talking about traffic generated to you. We're not talking about people that come in through the door necessarily. We're talking about follow-up that happens when the person finds you; you need a follow-up strategy whether or not the contact is initiated by phone, email, or online via the website.

When a new client gets to your website and chooses to give their name, phone number, and email address, they go into your funnel. Your funnel is the resource you have where you capture your leads and market to them specifically from there.

The reason for this is that they've gone through the trouble of giving you this information—they're a "warm lead" and obviously interested, and you have to get to them fast! The whole function of the funnel is to provide you with a resource that enables this sort of rapid response to whatever communication the client happened to initiate.

The best way to do this is to set up a basic autoresponder system. This system will provide two things to you: it's going to alert you that someone's given you information, and it's going to send them a message immediately. There are a couple of ways to do this, and later on we'll talk about different techniques including texting and direct voicemail. The most traditional and common auto response, however, is an email—that's something they should be getting immediately. A typical auto response email could look something like this:

Hi Mark,

Somehow not all vanilla ice-cream is created equal. In fact, in my opinion, there are plenty of cartons that shouldn't even be allowed to call themselves vanilla.

Finding the right attorney to help you can be like picking out vanilla ice-cream for the 1st time...

You are not 100% sure you are getting what you need for the situation you have.

Sometimes what you really need is more information before you make any decision.

There is a reason you still have not made any decisions and my report may not have answered all your questions. I find that every situation is a little different and I would almost 100% guarantee that your personal situation is unique and needs answers beyond what you already have.

Of course there are not enough hours in a week for me to talk to everyone with a question, and I wish I could, so I can't say that I will be able to connect with you today, but give my office a call and ask for when the next opening is on our firm's calendar.

We can spend 15 minutes on the phone and a lawyer from our firm will personally answer questions you have about elder law and working with attorneys.

Just tell the person that answers that I sent you this email and said it was ok that we scheduled a call this week or next.

We are here to help you with this process. Until we talk to you, have a great day.

All The Best,

That's an example of something they should be getting immediately after they submit their information on your web page. There are many services out there that provide these types of auto responding systems: Constant Contact, AWeber, InfusionSoft, Instant Customer, etc. Whichever service you go with, you have to make absolutely sure that they have a system in place capable of capturing names, storing names in an organized way, and making it as easy and automated as possible to send out those autoresponders.

You also need to have a strategy in place for phone numbers. If someone gives you their phone number, you should not only email them right away, but also email someone in your office right away a note that says "Hey, this person called interested in this. Here's their number." The reason for this is that the Internet is 24 hours; it doesn't close, it's always open, and your website is happily receiving visitors all around the clock. Your office hours, however, are only during the day; if your office hours are nine to four, for example, you won't be answering phones at ten in the evening.

The reason for emailing your office member is that if somebody comes in at night and submits their information, they get an immediate email; when your person gets in the next morning at nine, they can see the email and know someone tried to get in touch. They can then pick up the phone and say "Hey, this is Bob Jones from Jones, Smith, and Johnson. I saw you downloaded our special report- I hope it helped you out. I'm just calling to ask if there's anything we can help you with." This is a very personal follow-up to a warm lead, with an emphasis on the personal. We can't stress that enough—you're a local business providing a service to the community and you need to reach out and make those personal connections. The bigger the step, the better; an automated email is the minimum bar to entry. If they've gone through the trouble of giving you their email, you need to say thanks, email back, and throw in a special report; maybe email them again a few days later with another message. These should be automated; you can have a few templates for these emails that you can send out to your warm leads.

It's very important to implement this email / phone call system and use it regularly. This isn't e-commerce, and we're not going to close any deals online; there's no shopping cart, no impulse buy button that's going to magically give you clients without any legwork. You are still a local business, and we're engaged in local Internet marketing- you can't just send out email and expect things to happen.

You need to get that phone call or office visit to seal the deal!

Another good best practice is to email out one of your blog posts per month. Just take one of your blog posts per month, any one of them, and fire it out to anyone on your email lists. It's very easy to send out what's called a "broadcast message" to anyone on your email list still marked as open to receiving communication from you. The reason you want to do this is that, on the whole, this Internet marketing strategy is a long-term strategy; your clients may be thinking they need legal services but they may not need them quite yet. That doesn't mean, however, they won't need them down the line, and these periodic emails will let them remember who you are. This is called "top of mind awareness" in marketing; you want to be on the top of the mind to a client down the road. They may one day think "Oh! My dad needs info about his VA benefits. I've been getting these emails from a business down the road who deal with this sort of thing. Maybe I'll give them a call and see if they can answer my questions!"

Just The Facts:

* Follow-up is important, but it's equally important that your follow-up process be automated: no one should be sending out newsletters or follow-ups by hand, nor adding anyone manually to lists.

* Don't just follow-up with your leads when they fill out a form: follow-up in the office as well. This lets an employee call the lead as soon as possible, while they're still warm, and shows the lead that you're friendly and ready to do business.

* It's important to keep regular contact with your clients: fire off a blog post once a month to your email lists, in order to keep your business at the top of their minds.

9 THE BALANCE SHEET: HOW TO TRACK YOUR RETURN ON INVESTMENT (ROI)

In typical advertising solutions that we've seen from clients, most of the ad dollars get spent in the Yellow Pages along with some TV and some radio; these make up the vast majority of advertising budgets with clients that we've worked with. They're usually not spending too much money online, and if they are, it's an extension of the Yellow Pages that's usually not well-tracked and often very ineffective.

Advertising online, however, has a huge advantage over traditional advertising methods normally used by most businesses: it's extraordinarily easy to track what's going on throughout the entire online process.

You can track pretty well what's happening in each stage of the game: who emailed, what's in the funnel, what's going on, etc. and so forth. This is very difficult to do with regular advertising; quite often, the only method of communication that traditional advertising media gives a client is a phone number. Unless you're asking them where they heard about you or you're creating a unique phone number for each ad (which is, by the way, a very good best practice; more on that later), you're not getting very good information at all about how your advertising budget is helping you!

In contrast to these traditional advertising methods, you can glean vast amounts of data from the Internet and the tools available to you. You can track how many people visit, and what keywords they typed in that led them to clicking your site. If they visit your Google Places / Google + Local page, you can have instant knowledge there, including who visited, when, and how. Some directory listings have tracking data in place as well; the big Kahuna in this realm, however, is Google Analytics.

Google Analytics is an absolute must-have for your website. If it's not already on your website, ask your webmaster to integrate Google Analytics with your site; if he can't, it's time to find another webmaster. That's how important Google Analytics is to your ROI (Return on Investment). It tells you who's visiting, who's clicking, what data they're entering, how well your website is converting leads, how long your clients stay on your site, and more!

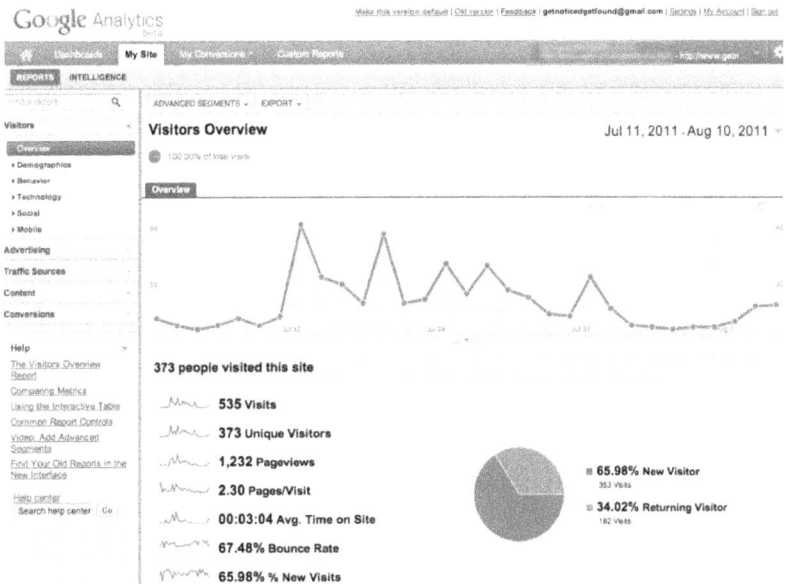

It's an absolutely essential tool for monitoring your ROI and your website, and it needs to be there.

Ok, so once again, you're in the business of selling your products and services right? You're not an online marketing geek. While tracking hits and calls is super important (you do need to know where your money is going), we found that most business owners just don't have the time to do this on a consistent basis. That's why for our private clients, we implemented a system where we track all traffic on their website...and all of the calls to the office. Then at the end of the month, they get a detailed report on all of the action.

We mentioned above having different phone numbers for each ad; even that is more easily tracked online. There are services online that allow you to create different unique forwarding numbers that all forward to your actual number; the only difference is that the call statistics are online and you can easily see at a glance how many calls each number received. This isn't to say you have to get rid of your current phone number—in fact, you shouldn't.

These numbers are only forwarding numbers and nothing more; clients with your old number can still get through perfectly fine.

Another great tool is Google Webmaster Tools, specifically because it tells you how many people are linking to you across the Internet and thus how well your Internet marketing strategy is doing overall. This should be complemented by statistics on your email funnel and autoresponders—you should be able to see how many people are getting / opening your emails and keep track of that as well. On top of all that, there's your own internal CRM (Customer Relationship Management system): how much money you're charging, how long you're working, how long you spend with each client, etc. and so forth. As we'll see, that's an incredibly key resource in determining your ROI.

On that note, we're assuming that you already have an internal CRM in place—it is crucial for this process and others. Discussing the process and tools to manage internal CRM is beyond the scope of this book, and there are many resources available to provide you help and support with implementing your own CRM; it's a vital step in the chain, and you need to have one before you can accurately calculate your ROI.

There are an almost unlimited number of things you can track online in order to measure your ROI, and if you're going to take anything away from this section it is this: it's imperative that you have a strong, stable, well-defined system in place in order to correctly track your ROI.

Most of the clients we work with believe they have a process in place, but when it's subjected to a rigorous examination it turns out that it breaks down. It's a good step that they even have a system in place—it's good sense and a standard marketing practice.

They're spending money, and they want to know where that money's going and how that money's helping them. For an Internet marketing strategy, however, you need to go above and beyond: you need to be taking in the data that show you the point of entry for all your clients.

An example monthly run down might look something like this: in total, 155 people visited our site this month. Of those visits, 35 came from Google Places / Google + Local, 120 from Google organic search, and 12 from Facebook fan pages. Of these 155 visits, we followed up with all of them; of the clients we followed up with, we closed 45, and each one of them was worth $1200 on average.

This is very basic, and the numbers are simply example numbers, but it should give you an idea of how you should be looking at and tracking your Internet marketing strategy.

This allows you to really get an accurate sense of valuation from clients that find you online: Are they worth the same amount as clients who found you driving by, or from referral?

We want to make sure you're capturing ROI information from those clients online, and these are extremely important statistics for you to know. Very often, we end up having to build new systems and processes for clients to get this reporting accurate; make absolutely sure that when planning out your overall Internet marketing strategy, you decide what metrics you're going to use and just how you're going to track them!

We can't stress this point enough: it's vital that you have an understanding of your ROI online all the time.

Efficient and accurate monitoring in this realm gives you an unparalleled advantage over traditional media; you can know down to the dollar whether spending in the online arena is good for your ROI.

In fact, we tell most of our clients that if they're not getting at least three times their ROI on their Internet marketing that something is really wrong. Usually, it's more than that; three times the ROI is our bare minimum for clients to see. If you're not getting that, it means something's wrong and you need to go back and look again at your strategy.

Either you've missed something along the way, or you're in a really competitive market and you need to bring in a second opinion or another expert to help you break into the market.

Tracking your own ROI also gives you another advantage: should you choose to hire a marketing agency for your Internet marketing, you can tell whether or not the marketing agency you hired is working well or not, and you can know whether you should stick with them or find someone new.

TIP: If you're working with an agency, you should absolutely require them to provide you with these ROI reports. They can get them, and if they're not giving them to you or claim they're unable to get them there's something seriously wrong; they're either hiding something or they're simply not as good as you thought they were!

Understanding your ROI, understanding your Analytics, using online-only phone numbers; all of these things simply underscore a philosophy that you should always adhere to in your online Internet marketing strategy: use every tool and resource available to you to know where your dollars are going and whether or not your online advertising dollars are really pulling their weight. The more control you have over your information flow and tracking information, the more valuable your online strategy is going to be and, ultimately, the more valuable your business as a whole will become!

Just The Facts:

* ROI tracking on print and TV ads is scarce and ineffectual at best: online ROI tracking offers a wealth of information, and enables you to very precisely track where your money is going and how much of it is coming back.

* It's imperative that you have a strong, stable, well-defined system in place in order to correctly track your ROI. Know where your money is going, know what sites are giving you hits, and know what percentage of leads you're converting, from which sites, and how much you're converting them for on average at the very least!

* If you work with a marketing agency, it's vital that they give you these ROI reports: they can give them, and if they can't or don't want to, something is seriously wrong.

10 WHAT IS MY NEXT STEP?

If you've reached this chapter, give yourself a pat on the back: you've done more for your online Internet marketing strategy than many local businesses will ever do.

You've got a very, very solid foundation for pulling clients in from the web; you're ranked high with a no-nonsense website that calls to action, you're a Facebook and Twitter regular, and you have in place a sophisticated system of follow-ups and ROI tracking that will enable you to pinpoint your highest-profit channels with incredible accuracy.

That's no reason to get complacent, however: the Internet is, by its very nature, a fast-moving target. Internet marketing isn't always going to stay in stasis, and you'll have to work to keep up with it. With that in mind, this chapter is dedicated to what's coming up down the road: things that aren't yet a major player in online marketing, but absolutely will be down the line. These are things that a local business has to think about; new technologies and trends that will have to be incorporated into your marketing strategy in order to keep at the top of your game!

Mobile

We've held this particular topic to the very end, but this is perhaps the most immediate of all the coming challenges for Internet marketing. Mobile devices are rapidly becoming the primary mode of interaction with the Internet; Mary Meeker of Morgan-Stanley has recently estimated that, given current mobile trends, the number of mobile devices that connect to the Internet will eclipse that of regular desktop PCs and laptops by mid-2013. You heard that right: by 2014, more people will be connecting to the Internet by phone than by computer.

In fact, mobile is already a driving force behind many of the search engine changes we've seen. Google is setting up its local places infrastructure because it believes information is going mobile. Mobile search is a different creature than traditional search; it's more often an immediate need. Users who search mobile are typically driven by an "I need something right now that's near me" mentality, as opposed to a more research-oriented desktop user who's more willing to sift through answers and Wikipedia articles. Very few people will be doing that on a mobile phone; most likely they're looking for a business nearby they can walk or drive to quickly.

This is great news, even for any local business, although many have looked skeptically at us when we've said this. Very often, people are out at lunch, driving around, or talking about stuff and think of their problem. More and more, they'll just think to themselves "Oh! I'll just use my phone really quick and search for an answer". The same applies to sitting around eating dinner or watching TV; chances are they have their iPhone, Android phone, or tablet sitting right next to them. Instead of waiting and looking up the answer to their problem later, they'll just pick up their mobile device and look up the answer right then and there.

This might seem far-fetched, but it's actually not: think about your own mobile smartphone use, or the usage patterns you've observed in others. There's a clear aura of instant gratification with any sort of mobile device, and users take advantage of it and get an instant answer. If your site's not mobile-friendly or your Google Places / Google + Local page is non-existent (Google Places / Google + Local is extremely mobile friendly) you're going to get left out in the cold.

The mobile realm also tightens up the ranking requirements quite a bit. On the regular desktop Internet, you've got to be in the top 7 ranking; it'd be nice to be in the top 3 or 4, but 7's the bare minimum. On mobile devices, if you're not top 2 you're not being seen; very few people scroll down on mobile phones, and often they simply tap the first or second result they see. This is important to you because mobile phones offer an unparalleled ease of use; for example, many phones like iPhone and Android offer built-in calling from the web. Users can simply tap a finger on your phone number and the smartphone dials the number automatically, without any need to ever pick up another phone. As mobile devices are more and more common, it's of critical importance that your site is mobile-friendly and sits in that A or B listing on Google's result returns!

Social

We've obviously covered a great deal of social media previously, and you're well-equipped to handle the social network scene at the moment. What we didn't cover, however, is the future of social networks- how they're going to change and how that's going to impact your overall online marketing strategy.

The first and most important aspect of future social is this: eventually, social media services are going to be more than just places where people connect. In the future, social media networks are going to transform into something more search engine oriented; people will go to Facebook not just to interact, but to search for things as well. This makes it crucial that you have an established presence early on. It is not too late, and you are not behind the curve: start now having presences on sites like LinkedIn, Twitter, Facebook, YouTube, StumbleUpon, Digg, and other social media sites. This doesn't mean you have to interact with all of these social media network every day or even frequently, though you're going to want to keep more in touch with the big ones as per the social network chapter. What you do want, however, is a presence; just make sure that your listings are in fact on these websites- you'll be very glad for it later!

Social networks are also getting very location-oriented as time goes on, so we can expect that trend to continue: this will eventually lead to a sort of social-mobile combo: users who are google searching while also in their Facebook mobile app. This is already a user pattern that exists, and we've noticed a rise in this user behavior recently; it's actually quite common now. Users are in the Facebook app and just go to the places listing and see what's around them. The first reaction is that this makes the most sense for restaurants and bars, and they've already start to capitalize on that, but this is useful for businesses as well: users will note "oh, this is where so-and-so office is" and they'll remember it. You need to have this local presence, because if you're not there and you're not found, someone else will be!

This social / search hybrid that we're seeing slowly creep up will also form another important piece of Internet marketing going forward: a combination of social word-of-mouth and Google ranking. Instead of letting Google figure out who's first, more people are going to go on Facebook and see what their friends think. Your interaction level, reviews, and presence on Facebook are going to be crucial at this stage of the game: more people are going to search there the way they're currently searching on Google. Some Internet results will still trickle through, but for the most part the results will come from the client's social networks.

This is important because people in general will take how their friends and family have viewed businesses very, very seriously: from a marketing perspective, it's a long-known and oft-proven fact that people give far more weight to opinions from friends and family than from any other source of marketing. As a result, this combo of social is search is going to be very influential, and you should keep an eye on it and stay on top of it as it progresses.

Direct Mail To Your Online List

You may wonder why I put direct mail in the " Next Step"

chapter; the fact is direct mail campaigns are the granddaddy of

internet marketing campaigns, but truth be told the techniques

we use in our online campaigns were derived from the same

strategies used in effective direct mail campaigns. It should be a

part of your overall marketing strategy too. Direct mail is

making a comeback. The reason for this is partly because of its

scarcity. Receiving mail every now and then, done properly, is

not a poor marketing option. It's not something you should rely

on heavily, but it's definitely something to keep in your arsenal

and use where it's appropriate.

If you already have a direct mail campaign going and want to

keep doing it, you need to find a way to incorporate Google

Places / Google + Local, Facebook, your website, or a call to

action in your direct mailers; you have to shift the goal to

getting people online. Direct mailing with mobile is an especially attractive option; being able to snap a picture and go straight to a website to see info or reviews or being able to text a certain number to get a special report are options that look very promising.

SMS Text Messaging

As mentioned with direct mailing, you can now have people text a number to receive information; they're actually entering your marketing funnel the moment they text that number. This is all automatic, too; you can have the same autoresponder system set up so that it sends texts in the same way that it sends emails. If a user puts in their mobile phone number, they get a text that says something like "We've received your name and email. Thank you very much for getting in contact! Check your email for a special report, free of charge. One of our representatives will be in touch!"

There is one other aspect about sms text messaging that needs to be addressed here: some in the hospitality industry (like pizza places and taverns) have automatic texts that send the latest coupons or deals: i.e. Tuesday happy hours, Five for Four Fridays, marketing specials to draw in business. It's effective in the hospitality business, but the same strategy can and does work with our client in other businesses as well. Depending on your product or service, this might work for you. Make sure to visit our website http://www.LocalOnlineAdAgency.com and stay up-to-date with our research in this area!

Once they give out their mobile phone number, don't be afraid to send out texts once or twice a month. Make sure the texts are useful, and don't send them more than once or twice per month; that could start to feel spammy for them. Texts are read over 90% of the time once received as opposed to emails, which are read only 17-20% of the time (and those are optimistic numbers). A well-placed, well-timed text or two every now and then can really help drum up some business and get some clients to call you!

Direct Voicemail

Direct voicemail is the practice of sending a voicemail directly to the phone without the phone ever ringing; this is possible to do now with mobile phone voicemail systems, and in actuality it works very well. These systems are quite nifty; you can set up outbound voicemails that talk about something new or something local that you and your business did. The voicemail can be about thirty to ninety seconds, and instead of calling you can send it directly to their phone. The voicemail notifier pops up but the phone never rings, meaning the client can see the voicemail message and listen whenever they want. It's non-intrusive and as a result the listen rate is much higher.

This is one of the reasons we recommended earlier to get mobile phone numbers from your leads; it not only opens up the texting avenue but the direct voicemail avenue as well.

The direct voicemail is very personal and very effective, and it's best used for events or other local things your business might

be doing. An example might be seminars- if your business does

seminars in the area about your topic, dropping a direct

voicemail to each of your clients is a great, personal way to let

them know about your upcoming seminars. It's easy, non-

intrusive, and works very well!

Summing Up

We called this chapter the "What's Next" chapter for a reason;

many of these technologies are going to or are already

beginning to affect the Internet marketing arena. In fact, some

of these ideas and strategies that we've talked about are

already coming into play. We've begun to experiment with

these things with some of our clients who are ahead of the

curve or are battling in very competitive markets, which

illustrates that these ideas are not simply theory or fluff. They're

real strategies that are beginning to come into the market, and

it's a good idea to keep abreast of them going forward.

Talk to an agency that you're working with and see what their ideas are on these future strategies. Nothing's set in stone with them, and a creative idea or two could really put you ahead in these arenas. It's also important that you find the right agency, one who specializes in these techniques; these aren't things your average webmaster will know how to do, and chances are an average webmaster hasn't even heard of them! Make sure you talk to an agency or service that thoroughly understands the full realm of Internet marketing, how it works with other marketing, and knowledge of future strategies down the line.

For more help, be sure to visit our website, INSERT-URL-HERE.com.

Just The Facts:

* Mobile and social media are going to be the driving forces in marketing over the next few years: both are driving marketing to be more location-oriented, due to the always-on nature that combines and unites mobile and social.

Keep up to date on them and don't miss any opportunities to be creative and capitalize on these markets!

* People give much stronger weight to opinions from friends: make sure you have a strong social presence, and leverage that social presence by having a well-established business that will rank high in the inevitable search / social hybrid arena.

* Direct mailing still has a place in the world, but it should be driving clients to go to your website in order to get that warm lead and—more importantly—get them to use a channel that's more easily tracked and analyzed.

* Don't ever be complacent: always think of new ways to innovate and incorporate new technologies, and make sure to work with agencies that have a good feel for the online field, are specialists in the online marketing world, and know how to help you stay at the top of your game.

11 RESOURCES & GLOSSARY

Find the RIGHT People to do this for you

The last thing you're going to need is a workforce. Let's face it, you didn't go to school, build your business, and teach your staff just so you could spend 11 hours a day uploading videos, submitting listings to directories, and designing websites.

Now we really wish we had better news for you, but finding competent people to do this work for you is not easy. Most web designers are broke, they know nothing about marketing, and many don't have any clients outside of your local city, and yes, they often live in their parent's basement. This is not the kind of person you can trust with your marketing budget so be thorough in deciding who to invest with.

We get asked all the time where to find a good web person. And our answer is that every time we find one who knows what they are doing (they are rare), we hire them to work on our team.

Outsourcing this work to India or to some fly-by-night business will cause more work than it will save.

And having one of your clerks or assistants do this work will drive you both crazy and possibly irreversibly ruin your working relationship.

You expect me to do all this AND run my business?

First, by now you'll agree, local web marketing is probably the most time-sensitive, urgent issue on your agenda right now. It doesn't seem like it at the moment, but when you look back on this book 6-18 months from now, you will probably wish that you had a time machine to get you back to this day.

The local Internet marketing door is WIDE open right now, but it is closing fast...and we would not want you to miss out on securing the financial future of your business just because you had a busy schedule.

On the other hand, it's very difficult to find good people to help you with your online presence. Most web designers are ignorant of conversion testing, and even if they do know how to build an effective website, it doesn't mean they know how to get your products and services on page #1 of Google multiple times. And outsourcing platform building of this kind to India or the Philippines will almost certainly mean you will end up having to fix the project because it wasn't properly executed, a senseless waste of time and money. (We use outsource workers for specific tasks, but language barriers and customs require training and supervision on an ongoing basis. Our project leaders are commission sales people dedicated to the continuing success of your campaigns and online platform).

We would love to offer the services of our marketing agency, but at the time of this writing, we are very busy with our current paying clients...and our commitment is to them.

In the interest of full disclosure, we provide a turn-key, 100% Done-For-You service which means you send us your business contact information and we do the rest. It's literally ALL done for you. Plus, we know how to get results faster than anyone. Our services are very expensive, and you will probably be able to find someone to do a bare-bones job for much less. But the way to look at it is: we invest a lot of money into our client's future. And, when you get 3, 5, or 9 more clients a month at $5,000.00 or more, we all win.

But we're restricting ourselves to only a handful of clients in any given geographical area. Your area may already be spoken for...and while that's not to say we won't take you, there's a good chance we will be committed already and have to pass.

Having said all of that, if you feel that you are a business that we should choose to work with and you would like to find out about my team's availability to help you and to get all of this DONE FOR YOU, please contact us at...

Phone: 1 (619) 722-3263
Fax: 1 (619) 466-6339
Email: Steve@OracularMarketing.com
Web: www.LocalOnlineAdAgency.com

We will, at the very least, be able to tell you if we are already working with a competitor in your area.

If we decide to move forward with you, we always start with a 22 Point Web Strategy Diagnosis. There is no obligation on either your or our part. This just begins the discussion as to how we may be able to help you. And while we know that some people take this experience-backed, high-quality web strategy then go and hire a cheap local marketing agency, we also know that the best customers, those who understand the value of growing their business by maximizing their online marketing investment will ask us to just "do it for me." We are looking for a small number of clients to build a long-term relationship with. And if that sounds like your business, then please feel free to write or call.

With that, we bid you adieu. If you've reached the end of this book, but you certainly haven't reached the end of how we can help you. If you've followed all the techniques and processes in this book and really took it to heart, you're very prepared to

wade into the online marketing arena and come out the victor;

you're ahead of most of your competitors and you have a clear

idea of what lies in store. Don't get complacent, be creative, and

you'll be successful in the online marketing arena for many

years to come!

APPENDIX A: GLOSSARY

ANALYTICS: Analytics are technical measures you can take to see what happens with visitors on your website: how long they stay, what they click, how many of them return to the website, and statistics of that nature. One of the best analytic software packages out there currently is Google Analytics, which is also free.

AUTORESPONDER: An autoresponder is a system put in place to automatically respond to communication initiated by a potential client, usually via email. Autoresponders can range from simple to extremely complex, and can either send just one generic email or choose from dozens of templates depending on the form used by the potential client or the information provided to the autoresponder by the potential client.

BING: A major search engine, like Google and Yahoo. It has many of the same features and has the next-largest market share of any of the search engines, after Google.

BLOG: Originally an abbreviation of the term "web log", it has now come to mean a type of website (or part of a website) that is frequently updated with new content and has many interactive options for users to leave comments and otherwise participate; many blogs are powered by software explicitly designed to make this frequent updating an easier and smoother process, like WordPress or Typepad.

CALL TO ACTION: Content on a website or other method of communication that appeals to the reader to contact the business.

CRM: An acronym for "Customer Relationship Management". In the context of Internet marketing, it most often refers to the software put in place that manages clients and potential clients of the business; names, locations, likes, dislikes, needs, and other information that the business may find relevant.

DIRECTORY: In the sense of Internet marketing, a website or part of a website whose purpose is to list businesses. Many of these, like Yelp, Merchant Circle, or CitySearch, also contain reviews of businesses that are often user-generated and submitted.

DUPLICATE CONTENT: Identical content that appears on multiple websites. Search engines have created ways of detecting this and often have algorithms that even detect if the content has just been altered slightly; content that has just be altered slightly and is still virtually identical to the original content will still be flagged as duplicate content by many search engines.

E-COMMERCE: The buying and selling of products and services over the Internet.

FACEBOOK: A social networking site that is currently the most popular in the world; it allows users to network with each other and socialize, including sharing photos, thoughts, status updates, and wall posts with each other.

FACEBOOK PLACES: A specific segment of the social networking site Facebook that allows users to see local spots around them as well as update their location in real-time from mobile phones or other means, allowing other users to see where they are at any given time.

GEOLOCATION: In Internet marketing and SEO, a term used to describe location-specific information; normally city and state for most local businesses.

GOOGLE MAPS: A part of Google's website that primarily deals with maps and navigation. One of the features of Google Maps is the ability for local businesses to list themselves on it, and the local search return feature was originally a part of this system. Google later integrated it into the main search system when it proved to be popular.

GOOGLE PLACES / GOOGLE + LOCAL: A part of Google's website that allows a business to have a specific page dedicated to them. It often hooks in with their location on Google Maps, and it features user-generated reviews of the business as well as links to other directories and review sites.

IP ADDRESS: A unique number that identifies a computer on a network.

KEYWORD: A term that a user searches against in a search engine to retrieve content that contains or is relevant to the term.

KEYWORD DENSITY: The use of a specific keyword present in any given piece of content. For example, given the keyword "racing" used five times in a 500-word blog post, the keyword density of "racing" would be 1%. Optimal keyword density is between 3 and 4%, and should not exceed 4% or it may be flagged as spamming.

KEYWORD PHRASE or LONG TAIL KEYWORD PHRASE: A phrase comprised of individual words but treated like a single keyword for the purposes of a search, like "whiter teeth dentist" or "teeth whitening Madison Wisconsin".

KEYWORD RICH: Content that has many keywords and uses them often, with good keyword density.

KEYWORD TOOL: Tools created to help select optimal keywords for search engine marketing, like Google's Keyword Tool. They often contain information such as amount of searches for a particular keyword and other metrics that help ascertain how popular or prevalent a given keyword or keyword phrase may be.

LINKEDIN: A social networking site that is geared towards businesses and professionals, enabling them to link up and network more effectively.

LOCAL SEARCH RETURN RESULT: A feature within Google's search engine that returns location-specific results for a user who types in keywords that relate to local businesses. For example, a local search return would appear for a user in Duluth, Georgia who typed in "emergency plumber." A map and local businesses that are relevant to the search result would appear in the ensuing search page.

NICHING: The practice of specializing your marketing strategy to a certain keyword or keyword phrase in order to rank in the highest spot in a local search return for that keyword or keyword phrase.

ROI: An acronym for "Return on Investment," which means the amount of profit; in literal terms, the amount of money returned for the amount of money invested.

SEARCH ALGORITHM: A series of computer algorithms used by major search engines to index, search, and rank websites on the

Internet.

SEARCH ENGINE: A website or company, like Google, Bing, or Yahoo, that indexes other websites on the Internet and allows users to enter keywords in order to find relevant websites.

SEO: An acronym for "Search Engine Optimization." It refers to the section of marketing that tries to increase exposure and clientele by using techniques and strategies to rank high on Internet search engines. Often interchanged with SEM (Search Engine Marketing).

SOCIAL MEDIA: Sites whose primary purpose is to enable users to share content with each other and socialize on the Internet; examples of websites that fall into this category are Facebook, Twitter, and LinkedIn.

SPAM: In Internet parlance, spam was originally used to refer to any unsolicited bulk messages sent over email. It is now also commonly used to refer to content on the Internet which is not useful and designed to make a page rank higher on search engines by tricking search engine algorithms into rating the content as more useful than it actually is.

TWEET: An individual post on Twitter.

TWITTER: A social networking service that allows users to post 140-character tweets to their account, with the ability for other users to follow them and respond to the tweets.

UNIQUE SELLING POSITION (USP): Unique Selling Position separates you from your competition in a specific market place. The term is often used to refer to any aspect of an object that differentiates it from similar objects.

URL: An acronym for "Uniform Resource Locator". It is the name that the user types into the browser bar in order to access a specific website; for example, "www.google.com" or "www.bing.com" would be examples of URLs.

ABOUT THE AUTHOR

Steven Laurvick is a Marketing Consultant, small business owner, author, real estate broker, and father. In 2002 he chose to end his career as a mortgage broker to build an online business which he continues to run and now uses as a laboratory to test market software systems, marketing applications, and online advertising methods. He is certified to teach software systems including Author Expert Marketing Machines, Instant Customer and Traffic Geyser. He is also a Google Engage specialist.

BRING US TO SPEAK AT YOUR NEXT EVENT:

Want to bring Steve Laurvick to speak at your next event?

Our programs are designed to optimize your businesses online marketing strategies. Our agency focuses on predictive internet marketing strategies and advanced SEO (Search Engine Optimization) and Local Search as an alternative means to traditional marketing.

Our X managing partners who perform this educational session have a combined experience of over 1,000 presentations. We have spoken at [insert speaking event examples]

Our Programs:

We offer several different programs including:

1) Websites, Google, and More: Getting Clients Online the Ethics, Pitfalls, and Techniques

2) Turning Clicks Into Clients: The Ultimate Presentation for Online Marketing

3) Social Media and Your Company: How to Leverage and Convert Clicks Into New Clients With Facebook, Twitter, LinkedIn, and Google+

This list changes from time-to-time depending on technology and demand. For a complete list of topics please contact us at [insert email address and phone number]

Inquire How You Can Book Us To Speak For FREE!

Every year our publisher subsidizes us to speak to a limited number of groups and associations at no cost to them. To inquire about having us speak at your event for no additional charge contact us at:

Steve@OracularMarketing.com

1 (619) 722-3263

Our books are found at the following booksellers.

-Amazon & Kindle

-Indigo

-Wherever fine books are sold

If you would you like to offer this book at your next event or association meeting, we offer quantity discounts. For more information please contact: Steve@OracularMarketing.com

BONUS!

Discover Exactly How You Can Make a Few Slight Adjustments and Begin to Dominate Local Search...It All Starts with Your 22 Point Review.

http://www.LocalOnlineAdAgency.com

If you want our valuable 22 Point Web Strategy Diagnosis visit this link. There is no obligation on either your or our part. This just begins the discussion as to how we may be able to help you. This URL gives you a coupon that makes this $400 review free for you, since you are reading and implementing the things in this book. Note, while it's free, we're busy, and availability may be limited. It's a great opportunity to get your online presence reviewed by one of our experts.

And while we know that some people take this experience-backed, high-quality web strategy then go and hire a cheap local marketing agency, we also know that the best customers, those who understand the value of growing their business by maximizing their online marketing investment will ask us to just "do it for me." We are always on the lookout for high quality clients to build a long-term relationship with. And if that sounds like your business, then please feel free to write or call.

Phone: 1 (619) 722-3263

Fax: 1 (619) 466-6339

Email: Steve@OracularMarketing.com

Oracular Marketing

by Steven Laurvick

ISBN 978-1-62735-008-2

9 781627 350082

5 2 8 5 0 >

Published by AME LLC